Andrew Raymond

Secrets of the Sphinx

☥

U N I Productions
REVEALER.COM

Josh
Thank you for your
"Inspiring" Letter.
my Best to you always
Love Andy ☥
9/15/97

Secrets of the Sphinx
Mysteries of the Ages Revealed
By: Andrew Raymond

Cover:
Lightbourne Images
Ashland, Oregon

Graphics:
New Vision Technologies Inc.
Nepean, Ontario, Canada
  Supplied over 50 Clip Art Graphics from:
  Presentation Task Force CGM V4.0
  Publisher's Task Force Volume 1
Micrografx-Windows Draw
Microsoft- Publisher & Design

Published by:
U N I Productions
P. O. Box 938
Paia, Maui, Hawaii 96779-0938

Publishers Cataloging-in-Publication Data
Raymond, Andrew
    Secrets of the Sphinx: Mysteries of the Ages Revealed /
    by Andrew Raymond.
        p.   cm.
Includes bibliographical reference.
ISBN 9646954-6-4
Library of Congress Catalog Card Number: 95-90407

About the Author

Born in 1942, Andy Raymond was raised and educated in rural Vermont. At the age of 18, he headed for the beaches of California and worked as an electrician. By the age of thirty, his quest for enlightenment caused him to "get light" and return to college for four years.

Andy graduated from Sonoma State University in California using the name "Rainbow" on his diploma to leave a permanent mark on his record. He did this to remind himself of the bliss he was experiencing while pursuing the wisdom of the ages, for he knew his desires would draw him into the lower material planes again.

Ultimately, Andy's search brought him to Hawaii. For over seven years, he conducted tours to some of the remote areas of Maui. On occasion, he would risk opening up to the tourists and sharing what he had learned about the workings of our solar system with its connections to our spiritual traditions.

Many of the tourists would inquire about sources for more information, and ask why he was not teaching in the universities. Andy would just grin like the Cheshire cat and reply: "Would you rather be by these waterfalls or under fluorescent lights in concrete buildings?"

The spiraling quest for knowledge and the acceptance of Andy's teachings by a majority of the visitors on his tours led to the birth of this book for all who want to know what was taught on the "Road to Hana".

Acknowledgments

The author wishes to thank Paul Wood, editor for Jungle Press on Maui, Hawaii for his encouragement and tutelage. His input has led directly to this publication. I also want to acknowledge Carol Ann Carlucci-Ostrover and Cliff Ostrover for the many hours they contributed to the creation of this book. I am also grateful to Jim Diamond and Phyllis Ellman for their guidance in this project. My love and gratitude goes out to the following families who have been intricately involved in my life at one time or another: Raymond; Tomasi; Danials; Thornton; Alafat; Carlucci; Davis; Fortier; Fox; Jay; La Cass; Lester; McCuen; Mitchell; O'Connor; Partlow; Schiwietz; Skaats; and Verzic. I also wish to thank all my friends, my acquaintances, and my co-workers at Ekahi Tours on Maui for their love and support over the years.

Table of Contents

Foreword

This book is designed for the inquisitive person who is pursuing knowledge on all levels. It will provide the seeker of truth an insight into some of the shrouded and paradoxical mysteries of life. We will explore a few major pieces of the universal puzzle and discover how they fit together using the cycle of the *great year* as a base.

This work is designed to assist people who are trying to make sense out of the religious, astrological, or secular philosophies that they may have come in contact with as a part of their natural development. We will combine a few of the more popular philosophies with our scientific knowledge to help us comprehend the overall revelation that is enveloping our planet at this juncture in the great year.

One needs a basic understanding of our previous teachings in order to put them to rest. By perceiving the esoteric knowledge hidden within these myths, people will no longer be bound by the limitations of the stories themselves.

After years of searching for the meaning of life, I came upon some scientific truths that allowed me to perceive the interrelationships between science, religion, and mythology. Finally I could make more sense out of many of the different philosophies being expounded all around me.

This publication is my means of passing on these insights that come from sources more advanced than I. Sharing what information I have uncovered completes this phase of my life.

I am not trying to be overly precise or technical in my use of dates and terminology, as there are hundreds of publications and sources of information available already on any specific area of interest this work may entice you to investigate. This material is designed to shed light and give each of us a renewed vitality in our own life's work.

At the least, this book should bring us to a point of communicating or disputing this kind of information intelligently. I only ask that you do it with love, as I am continually changing, balancing, and reorganizing my own beliefs with the information I am receiving from inside and outside myself.

Let us see what we can discover when we combine our data and look at it from a unique perspective.

1

Exploring the Year

U sing the medium of this publication, we are going to unravel some ancient mysteries that were woven into our myths, legends, and symbols as a means of preservation for a time when the masses will be ready to discover the wisdom they contain. In order that we may all start off on the same "paw" in our exploration of the Giza Sphinx and other cryptic riddles from bygone ages, we are going to review a few of the many astronomical cycles of our solar system that are always operating in full unison with us and our Creator.

We must understand the signs that are taking place outside ourselves if we are going to embark on a journey to comprehend the mythological symbols that have been implanted within our minds — because ultimately, they are one and the same. As Jason and the Argonauts, the ancient Egyptians, and the early Polynesians once set sail for uncharted lands using the stars as a navigational aid, we will also look briefly at the cycles of the celestial bodies to map our journey of discovery.

We would be foolish to belabor ourselves with an inspection of the 24-hour cycle of our planet, called a "day," because we observe this rotation of our Earth on its axis 365 1/4 times in one year. Instead, we are going to devote this chapter to a brief exploration into the causes and effects of an Earth year, which consists of one revolution of our planet around the sun.

After that, we will probe the 25,800-year cycle of our Earth that only a few of us take time to study, since our life span is but a drop in a bucket within the sphere of this greater year. Yet, people like Nostradamus, Plato, Revelations writers, geologists, and other scientists have used it to predict the impending changes that this spiraling cycle will inevitability cast upon us.

But first, let us recall what we know about our Earth year, so that we have a common base from which to launch our exploration into the *great year*.

As our Earth makes one yearly orbit around the sun, the 23 1/2 degree tilt in our planet's axis causes the focal point of the sun to swing like a pendulum on the surface of the Earth. This focal point travels north from the equator to the Tropic of Cancer, then south across the equator to the Tropic of Capricorn, and once again north to the equator. This yearly cycle produces our spring, summer, fall and winter seasons.

Every year, on or about March 21, the sun's focal point, or plane, passes over our Earth's equator as it travels north. We refer to this day as the *Vernal Equinox* or the *Spring Equinox.*

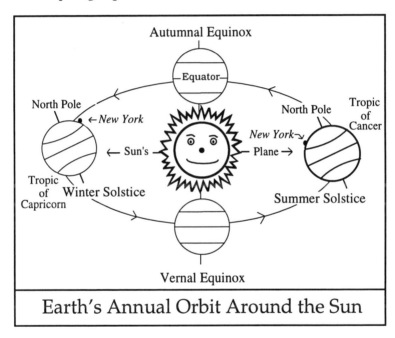

Autumnal Equinox

Equator

North Pole

← *New York*

← Sun's

Tropic of Capricorn

Winter Solstice

North Pole

New York ↘

Plane →

Tropic of Cancer

Summer Solstice

Vernal Equinox

Earth's Annual Orbit Around the Sun

The exact minute the sun's plane crosses the equator heading north is the exact minute the news media heralds as the first minute of spring in the Northern Hemisphere.

As the days pass, the sun's focal point keeps coming north. On or about May 27, because of the daily rotation of our planet, the high noon sun traverses all of the Earth's surface located on 21 degrees north latitude. This includes Maui, Hawaii; Guadalajara, Mexico; Hanoi, Vietnam; and Nagpur, India.

If you place a stick straight in the ground on 21 degrees north latitude, the sun's plane will be directly above the stick around noon time, and there will be no shadow cast by the stick. The local news media and the residents of Maui call this a shadowless day.

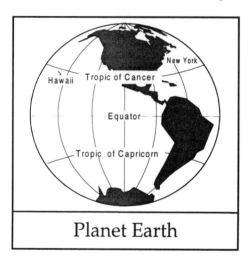

Planet Earth

It is around this time of year that people, who are not accustomed to the vertical rays of the high-noon sun, receive the worst sunburns in the shortest exposure times, because the sun's rays are coming straight through the atmosphere. The amount of atmosphere the sun's rays pierce to reach us varies with the penetration angle. This is the same reason that we can look directly at the sun during the last few minutes of a sunset.

For the remainder of the spring season, the sun's focal point continues moving north day by day, until it reaches the *Tropic of Cancer* on or about June 21. On every map and globe, we depict the Tropic of Cancer as a line encircling the Earth at 23 1/2 degrees north latitude. This is just north of the Hawaiian Islands, passing through Mexico, Northern Africa, and India.

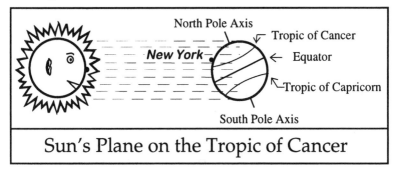

North Pole Axis
Tropic of Cancer
New York
Equator
Tropic of Capricorn
South Pole Axis

Sun's Plane on the Tropic of Cancer

Just as the sun's plane comes overhead on the Tropic of Cancer, the Earth starts to tilt back, the sun appears to stand still for one minute, and many people celebrate "sun-stand-still day" or *Summer Solstice*. The exact minute the sun appears to stand still is the precise time the news media gives us for the first minute of summer.

Then the summer sun starts heading south again. It crosses over Maui in the middle of July, providing the island with another shadowless day. It crosses the equator on or about September 22. Although the residents of both hemispheres refer to this moment as the *Autumnal Equinox,* the people living in the southern

13

hemisphere call this crossing their first day of spring. The autumnal sun keeps traveling south, until it reaches the *Tropic of Capricorn* around December 21.

We illustrate the Tropic of Capricorn, on Earth maps and globes, as a line encompassing the earth on 23 1/2 degrees south latitude. That line cuts through Australia, South America and the southern tip of Africa.

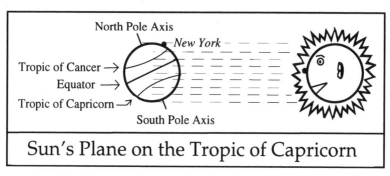

North Pole Axis

New York

Tropic of Cancer →

Equator →

Tropic of Capricorn →

South Pole Axis

Sun's Plane on the Tropic of Capricorn

When the autumn sun reaches the Tropic of Capricorn, the Earth's axis has also reached the opposite extreme in its tilt relative to the sun's focal point or plane. The sun appears to stand still for one minute, and we celebrate the first day of winter or the *Winter Solstice* in the northern hemisphere. This is the shortest day of the year for those people living north of the equator.

As our globe starts to tilt back, our winter sun continues heading north, for the next three months, towards its next crossing of the equator. This crossing on March 21 will provide us with a new first day of spring or Vernal Equinox.

An *equinox* or *equinoctial point* is the exact point at which the plane of our sun intersects the plane of our celestial equator, giving us equality of day and night.

This balance of day and night at the equatorial or equinoctial regions of our Earth also affects the growth of the plants and the kinds of animals found at any location on our globe. Of all the types of plants and animals living on our planet, 67 percent of them reside within a few thousand miles of the equator.

Life on the Equator

If we have seen every type of plant and animal in the northern and southern hemispheres, excluding this narrow band at the equator, we have seen only 33 percent of the types of plants and animals in the world.

A plant or a tree that flowers two months in New York might bloom four months in Hawaii, and six months at the equator. At 21 degrees north latitude on Maui, the thimbleberry bushes have blossoms and berries on the same branch all year long. When we take that plant to a place like New York City which is located near 41 degrees north latitude, the plant is bare in the winter. It blossoms in the spring, it produces berries in the summer, and it becomes barren once again in the fall.

In the equatorial regions of our Earth, just the opposite happens. We have berries and blossoms on the same plant all year long, and they are even larger than the ones growing in Hawaii.

Any image one has of living in a garden on Earth and eating fruit off the plants all year long could become a reality in the equatorial regions of our planet.

It should also be obvious that anyone who likes a little spice in his or her life would live away from the equinoctial regions of our globe, because the further away from the equator one chooses to live the more intense the four seasons become.

Should we move to Alaska, we can have thirty-foot tides combined with six months of day and six months of night. When we live on the equator, we find that the tide shift is small, and the hours in a day and night are close to being even throughout the year.

In one of the mythological stories of creation, we have *Eve* as the balance of Adam or man. We use the word "<u>eve</u>ning" to refer to the equilibrium between day and night. The word "<u>eve</u>n" means to "<u>leve</u>l," to balance, or to make straight.

16

The suffix "-ator" is also involved in this play on words. It means one who causes, a doer, or an actor. Hence, we perceive the word "cre<u>ator</u>" as one who causes or brings into being, and the word "equ<u>ator</u>" as the balance point or central focus of our sun that causes almost everything to grow.

The equatorial regions of our Earth receive the most even or balanced distribution of our sun's energy throughout the year.

I believe it would be fair to say that the more balanced we are on any level of existence, the more the universe rewards us by making life temperate. The significance of the yin & yang of life should become clearer to us as we progress through the pages of this book.

Now that we have examined the balance of nature within the cycle of the year, let us move on to the next chapter, where we are going to examine a larger cycle of our Earth. This greater cycle is veiled in folklore and legends, because we are too steeped in our short life span to remember this cycle of our planet with its poignant effects on us.

2

The Platonic Year

In order to uncover some of the mysteries that are shrouded in our mythological and religious symbols, including the Giza Sphinx, we must look beyond our Earth year to a much longer cycle of our planet.

We call this greater cycle, or one wobble of the Earth, the Platonic year in honor of the Greek philosopher Plato — whose ideas concerning the realities of the physical and metaphysical planes are still cherished by many of us who are seeking the wisdom of the ages.

I am going to introduce this cycle in the simplest way possible, as we only need a general knowledge of it to comprehend the wisdom this book intends to impart.

The combined gravitational effects of the sun, moon, and planets on the Earth's equatorial bulge cause the Earth's axis to sway clockwise in a slow circle, like the motion of a spinning top.

It takes 25,800 years for the Earth's axis to complete one wobble, sway, or clockwise circle. This 25,800-year cycle is called the Platonic year. It is also referred to as the *precession of the equinoxes* or the *great year* in a comprehensive dictionary.

In our solar system, the Platonic year is one of the longest regularly recurring cycles that are well known to our astronomers.

The sun's plane crosses the equator each year on March 21, the day of the Vernal Equinox. At the exact location where the sun's plane crosses the equator, the sun would be directly above the equator at high noon, and it would be a shadowless day for people living in that area.

The cycle of the Platonic year causes the sun's plane to cross the equator about one mile west from where it crossed the year before. It takes around 25,800 years for the sun to go all the way around the equator and cross at the same point again.

When we take an imaginary line off the Earth's North Pole axis and extend it into the heavens, we find that the line points at a star that we call Polaris, our "North Pole" star. The cycle of the Platonic year causes the line off the North Pole to scribe a circle in the heavens approximately 25,800 years long.

Polaris will reach the point at which it comes closest to aligning with the North Pole axis of our Earth in the year A.D. 2105. In two thousand years, because of the effects of the Platonic year, there will be no Pole Star, as there was no Pole Star two thousand years ago.

The next North Pole Star after Polaris will be Al Deramin around the year A.D. 7500; later, Deneb will hold that position. Thirteen thousand years from now, the bright star Vega will be the North Pole Star again, as it was the North Pole Star nearly thirteen thousand years ago.

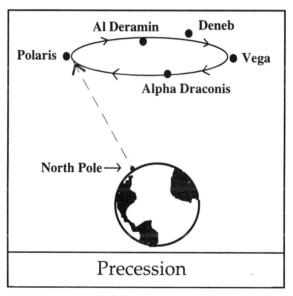

Precession

As the precession continues, Alpha Draconis, which is also known as the Dragon Star or Thuban, becomes the next North Pole Star after Vega around the year A.D. 21600.

21

Alpha Draconis aligns closer to the North Pole axis of our Earth than all of the other Pole Stars in a Platonic year. It is also the only Pole Star in the Platonic year to be in the exact position to shine down the Descending Passage of the Great Pyramid of Giza, because the Descending Passage is in true alignment with the North Pole axis of our planet.

In his book *The Great Pyramid Decoded,* Raymond Capt says, "the most precise alignment of the Dragon Star and the Great Pyramid occurred on the Vernal Equinox of the year 2141 B.C."

The imaginary line off the North Pole axis of the Earth moves away from Alpha Draconis as it continues to scribe its 25,800-year circle in the heavens. Around the year A.D. 27900, our North Pole axis will once again point at Polaris, where it is at this time in history.

We are going to continue learning about the Platonic year so that we can expose the secrets of the Giza Sphinx and many other ancient symbols in due time. In the meantime, don't let my planting of seeds, that need time to mature, bog you down. Just keep on moving. The overall message of this book is much simpler than the medium being used to deliver it to you.

The twelve constellations of the Zodiac were studied by the Egyptian, Hindu, Persian, Indian, Chaldean, Hebrew, Greek, and Chinese astronomers and astrologers. The circle formed in the heavens by these constellations is close to being aligned with our celestial equator. When the sun's plane crosses the equator on the first day of spring, we could ask ourselves which of the twelve constellations is out behind the sun.

At this time in history the sun appears, to an observer on Earth, to be located between Pisces and Aquarius on the first day of spring.

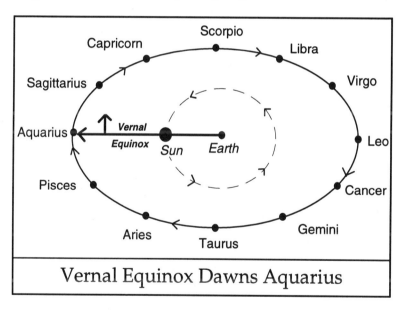

Vernal Equinox Dawns Aquarius

The Platonic cycle causes a slow backwards movement of the sun's apparent position in the Zodiac when viewed on successive Vernal Equinoxes. We refer to this slow-backwards movement as the precession of the equinoxes.

The sun's apparent position moves a little bit west in a constellation when observed on the same day each year; it takes an equinox sun approximately 2,150 years to transit one of the twelve constellations on its 25,800-year jaunt around the Zodiac.

At this point in history, the Vernal-Equinox sun is just entering Aquarius on the first day of spring. This is the scientific explanation for what we call the *Dawning of the Age of Aquarius* or a *New Age*.

If we were to check the sun's position in the Zodiac on successive Vernal Equinoxes, we would see that it will take approximately 2,150 years for the spring sun to travel through the constellation of Aquarius on its way to Sagittarius. If we were to live for 25,800 years, or one great year, we would witness twelve New Ages.

In the long view of things, the Earth has been at this place in the astronomical calendar thousands of times before, as each Platonic year *spirals* onward.

Consider the twelve star constellations of the Zodiac the same way we think about the twelve months in the annual cycle of our planet. The Earth year consists of twelve months of about thirty days in each month. In the Platonic year, there are twelve ages of nearly 2,150 years in each age.

The name of an age is taken from the name of the constellation that the Vernal-Equinox sun or the spring equinoctial point is traversing. When used correctly, the Zodiac is the master calendar or the face of a clock for the Platonic year.

Because there is no line in the heavens between the star constellations, we find all the different shamans on the planet quoting us a different time for the start of our impending New Age. Most people who are "into" this esoteric knowledge point to the year A.D. 2000, plus or minus 40 years, as the dawning of the Age of Aquarius.

Since such a gradual shift of ages is taking place, we will just welcome you to the *Dawning* of a *New Age*.

The astronomical ruins around the earth prove that the ancient shamans knew a lot more than we usually give them credit for. They understood not only the Platonic year but some subtle variations in its slow-working celestial mechanism.

For example, many of these observatories, including Stonehenge on England's Salisbury Plain, accurately record the 18.6-year cycle of the moon. This cycle causes every eclipse of the sun to repeat itself at a different place on the earth every 18.6 years. It also creates an 18.6-year wave or nodding in the precessional movement called *nutation*.

Should we try to trace the sun's vernal-crossing point as it moves about a mile west each year on the equator itself, we must look beyond this nutational cycle to discern any even pattern in its movement. However, when we observe the position of the sun in the Zodiac on successive Vernal Equinoxes, the westerly movement will appear "steady" as each year passes, because the stars and sun are too far away to be affected by the cycle of the moon.

Our ancient ancestors not only understood the patterns of the Platonic year but they also incorporated the reckoning of that long cycle in the designs of their great monuments. We shall explore some of these markers, including the Giza Sphinx, as we move through the chapters of this book.

Now that we have been exposed to Plato's year with its twelve ages, let us create an imaginary time machine that we may use to view some of our previous ages. Climb aboard, set the "year" knob for "slow reverse", push the "travel" button on the main control panel, and hold onto your head — we're out of here.

3

Glimpsing Back in Antiquity

For the last two thousand years, the Vernal-Equinox sun has been moving west through Pisces the Fish. During this period of time, many people on the planet have been drawing fish symbols in the sand and talking about the fisherman of souls. The fish is one of the more important symbols in Christianity. In the parables, Jesus feeds the multitude with a few small fishes.

The fish, however, is not just a Christian symbol. It is common to many cultures of the Piscean Age. The Greeks and the Romans maintained the fish symbol in reverence of the goddess of love, beauty, and fruitfulness who was born of the foam of the sea. She was known as Aphrodite by the Greeks, Astarie by the Phoenicians, and Venus by the Romans.

The word *Friday* comes from the Scandinavian name *Freya* that translates to Venus. The Pagans wouldn't eat fish on Friday in honor of Venus, while many Christians reversed that policy and kept Friday sacred by eating fish instead of meat.

Two to four thousand years ago, in the age before the Piscean Age, the Spring-Equinox sun was traveling west through Aries the Ram. When we look back in history, we see the Jewish rabbis putting rams' horns in the temples and lambs' blood on the doors. It was during this period of history that the astrologers noticed the Spring-Equinox sun was traversing the constellation of Aries.

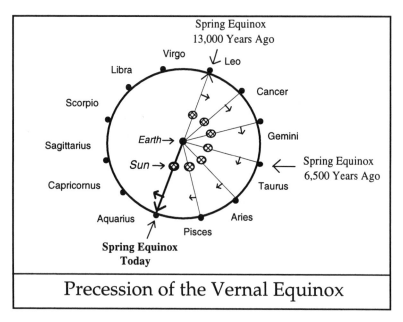

Precession of the Vernal Equinox

The constellation in which the Vernal-Equinox sun moves always indicates the name of our age and our position in the Platonic year or master calendar.

Therefore, the astrologers wrote down all the sun signs as they saw them 4,000 years ago, and they assigned Aries as first sign of the Zodiac.

In order that we may pick up some additional information for our journey through the ages, I am going to ask you to push the "Pause" button on our time machine's main control panel. Set the computer to "Related Information" and push the "Enter" button.

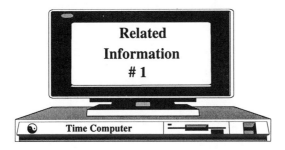

We can locate the sun's position in the Zodiac on the Vernal Equinox, or on any given day of the year, by going out in the evening and watching the sunset. When the stars become visible, we look into the heavens just above where the sun set and we can see which one of the twelve star constellations is shining. Then we look up a little higher in the sky and see which constellation is there. Now we can deduce which one of the twelve star constellations is out behind the bright sun.

For example, if we were to observe the constellation of Gemini in the evening sky just above where the sun set, we would also see Cancer a little above Gemini.

29

The constellation of Leo would be just above both of them. We can now deduce that the sun is in Taurus on this day, because the constellation of Taurus is just below the horizon where the sun just set.

It is only the rotation of the Earth that makes the sun and stars appear to rise and fall throughout the day. It is necessary to use this method to determine the position of our sun in the Zodiac, because we are unable to visually determine which stars are behind the brilliant sun.

Related Information # 2

If you wanted to examine how the different cultures aligned their calendars with the progression of the heavenly bodies, you could exhaust a lifetime in study.

Therefore, let us be satisfied with the knowledge that some of the ancient civilizations celebrated the start of the New Year at the exact minute of the Vernal Equinox. Many modern cultures, including some countries of the Middle East (not to mention our farmers), still observe this time as the unofficial beginning of their New Year.

We ourselves placed the New Year in spring until more recent times. Julius Caesar moved the first day of the New Year to January when he introduced the Julian calendar on January 1, 45 B.C. We notice that some of the names of our months still reflect March as the first month of the year. October is eight, November is nine, and December is ten.

In olden days, the beginning of spring was the official start of the New Year in the English calendar. It wasn't until 1751 that the English Parliament enacted a law to move the beginning of the New Year from March 25 to January 1, 1752.

By then, our calendars were already unsynchronized with the position of our heavenly bodies, because the precession of the Vernal-Equinox sun had already moved from Aries to Pisces. These later decrees increased the inaccuracy of our calendars even more by moving the start of the New Year from the beginning of spring to January 1.

It will become evident to us as we advance through this work that many of our great monuments, mythologies, and legends reckon themselves by using the first day of spring as their marker or point of origin.

Related Information # 3

One of the reasons the astrologers and the astronomers have some difficulty communicating with each other is as follows. On the first day of spring, the astrologers start professing "The Sun is in Aries!" "The Sun is in Aries!" The astronomers shake their heads in disbelief, as they know the Vernal-Equinox sun has been traveling through the constellation of Pisces, the Fish, for the last two thousand years.

At this time in the Platonic year, the Spring-Equinox sun is dawning into Aquarius. Strange as it may seem, many of us are still telling everyone born on March 21 that they are an Aries. All of our birth signs are off by nearly two constellations.

For example, when my father looked out into the heavens while I was being born on May 17, 1942, the sun was near the end of Pisces and expected to arrive at Aries around May 21, 1942. Anyone who looks into the heavens, rather than a book or a newspaper, to determine my birth sign will perceive that I am really not a Taurus.

Around 4,000 years ago, all of our birthday-sun signs and the constellations of the Zodiac coincided. Through unintentional neglect, all of our sun and moon signs have been allowed to slip out of touch with our present astronomical reality.

When we read an astrological calendar, it may tell us the *moon* is in Taurus, the Bull, tonight. When we look at the stars, however, we find the moon more than a constellation away from the horns of Taurus (which resemble a large "V" between Orion's Belt and the Pleiades).

Why should I be calling myself a Taurus if the sun was really in Pisces the day I was born? It appears that teaching the population something that isn't true is much easier than going through the complex task of updating our antiquated systems.

If I am an eternal soul, why am I bothering to bind myself to the day I was birthed into this temporary body anyway?

"Where's that Sun?"

Sure, the astronomical bodies of the heavens have an influence on us, as everything in the universe is inter-related. Therefore, it may be time for us to start using the Zodiac as a master calendar rather than a tool to spell us into thinking we are something that we really are not.

Okay! When you feel you are ready to continue looking back through the ages, put the time machine's "year" control on "auto". Set the computer to give us additional information as needed, and set the "squawk" transponder to "friendly" in case we encounter any UFOs. Now, push the "resume" button on the main control panel. These settings should guide us through the remainder of this book.

"Ready Mates?"

Four to six thousand years ago, the sun was traversing through Taurus, the Bull, on the first day of spring. When we look back in history, we find the Egyptians, Cretans, Hindus, and others paying homage to the sacred cow during this age.

When we study the ancient Egyptian calendars from around 4000 B.C., we find that they divided the year into twelve months of thirty days each. Because twelve times thirty only accounts for 360 days, the

Egyptians had to insert five sacred-feast days at the end of each year to reckon their calendar with the solar calendar that has 365 1/4 days in a year. Even with this adjustment, their calendar still gained one full day every fourth year because of the extra quarter of a day in the solar year.

The very early Egyptians celebrated the start of the New Year on the day Sirius, the brightest star in our heavens, first appeared on the eastern horizon at sunrise. When the masses throughout the land could see the bright star Sirius shining through the dawning sky, they knew the sun was entering Taurus, because Sirius is very close to Taurus in the heavens.

This was a fairly accurate indicator of the start of the New Year, and it was much easier than dropping the ball in New York's Times Square. All of Egypt could see for themselves that it was Happy New Years and the beginning of spring.

Even though later Egyptian calendars start the first day of the New Year on the Autumnal Equinox, the Egyptians still paid homage to Taurus the Bull on the first day of spring.

It was most likely during the five feast days, before the start of the new year, that Moses came down from the hill and said to his exiled followers: *Get that golden bull out of here, and put some lamb's blood on the doors. The sun is now entering Aries on the Vernal Equinox. I can't believe you are so blind that you can't see what's taking place in the heavens.*

We went grudgingly from Taurus to Aries.

"I'm sorry, but your age is over."

Moses Replaces Taurus with a Ram

Six to eight thousand years ago the spring sun was moving through the constellation of Gemini the twins. Gemini is also known as Adam and Eve. This coincides with the period during which most Biblical scholars say Adam and Eve would have lived on Earth. Even the 8,000 year old Egyptian Zodiac, in the Temple of Denderah, shows the Vernal-Equinox sun in the constellation of Gemini.

We note the Old Testament is full of star names. People followed stars for births. Job 9:9 says, *"He made Arcturus (the Bear,) Orion, the Pleiades and the constellations of the south."* It also refers to the twelve constellations of the Zodiac or the Mazzaroth in Job 38:32

which says, *"Do you have the power to bring forth the Mazzaroth in their season or guide Arcturus with his sons?"*

Can it be true that the Old Testament is also an astronomical record of the last four ages that we are just completing, and that the prophecies of Revelations, Edgar Cayce, Nostradamus and the American Indians are all hinting at the expected changes associated with the coming of Aquarius the Man?

Wisdom of the Ages

We will delve over our heads into prophecies in a later chapter, but for now, I would like to reiterate that it has been over 2,000 years since the Spring-Equinox sun left the constellation of Aries, and we are still shackled to that poor Ram.

Even our ancient predecessors kept updating the master calendar throughout the ages. The ancient

Egyptians moved the calendar age from Gemini to Taurus, Moses moved it to Aries, Jesus tried to move it to Pisces, and "we" are going to move it to Aquarius. Thank God that Moses or the Shepherd isn't around here today kicking butts, because only a few of us would be able to sit down right now. It is time to update our knowledge.

In closing, I just want to let you know that I am really enjoying my part in creating this book, and I hope you can feel the humor and love in which it was created. Otherwise, I could be the only one standing at the table.

I have to admit, though, that getting my buns tanned would be much better than another inquisition or a good burning at the stake.

Let us move on, as this chapter is now history. The next one awaits us with some more revealing information.

4

Ancient Cults, Easter, and Spring

B efore we go any further, we need to look at the word *cult.*

I wanted to title this chapter "Ancient Cultures, Easter, and Spring," but the title looked too big and out of symmetry with the heading for "Chapter 4." I had reservations concerning the use of the word cult, because I would not want people running around the planet calling this a cult book.

Let us dispel any misinformation we may be possessing about this word right here and now:

The word "cult" ordinarily refers to a specific system of religious worship or devotion — with special attention paid to its observances, ceremonies, and rites. A cult is usually focused on an extravagant devotion to a person, cause, or thing. It is also a religion or sect whose followers are considered to be false, unorthodox, or extremist by the dominant religions.

If we apply this definition fairly, we find that "cults" include some mighty respectable company, including Paganism, Buddhism, Druidism, Catholicism, Hinduism, Protestantism, and Confucianism. Most of these beliefs contain cultured people who are possessing a good education, refinement of mind, exemplary morals, and fine taste.

Enough said!

We need to discern how important the Vernal Equinox is to a few of the many cultures who use it before we continue looking back at the different ages in our Platonic year. This will help us understand all the secrets that are being unraveled as we progress through this book.

Most of us are aware of the ancient megalithic monuments that began to appear in Spain and Western Europe around 3000 B.C. In England, for example, the megalithic builders created a precise astronomical observatory called Stonehenge to follow the movements of the heavenly bodies.

We all know about the Mayan and Aztec cultures, who built great pyramids and observatories to find the Spring Equinox and to follow the astronomical movements in the heavens. The Maya are best remembered for their development of a very accurate astronomical calendar, and for their use of writing.

Mayan Civilization

The temple the North American Indians built in Arizona is one of the oldest astronomical observatories on the North American continent. The four-story structure has two holes in the east wall to follow the annual transit of the sun through the Spring and Fall Equinoxes. It also has two holes in the west wall to follow the Summer Solstice and the 18.6 year nutational cycle of the moon.

Scientific documentation shows the alignment of these openings to be quite accurate. The park rangers at *Casa Grande Ruins National Park* in Coolidge, Arizona, believe the observatory was constructed by a prehistoric culture, known as the Hohokam. This highly developed society built the observatory, hundreds of miles of irrigation canals, and other structures between A.D. 300 and A.D. 1450.

41

Let us place all the ancient cultured people, who left us mysterious ruins strewn across the planet, in a revered place in our hearts and move on to just one of the many ancient temples that has survived to this modern day.

The Vatican in Rome has the *Room of the Four Winds*, and on the east wall there is a hole to let the sun shine onto a marble floor. When the solar beam hits the small circle on the marble floor, it tells the Vatican that today is the Vernal Equinox and the sun is crossing the equator.

In the year A.D. 1582, the Vatican astronomers brought Pope Gregory XIII up to the Room of the Four Winds. They showed him that the solar beam was hitting the small circle and, therefore, that this day was the first day of Spring. The astronomers also noticed that the Julian Calendar listed this as March 11, 1582 — not March 21, as it should have been.

The calendar had slipped by ten days since the year A.D. 325 when the Council of Nice had made March 21 the official calendar date for the first day of spring.

The sunbeam, of course, was correct. It was in perfect alignment with the sun indicators of the Egyptians, the Greeks, the Hindus, and the Persians. The Julian calendar had already slipped ten days behind the solar calendar because of the precession of the equinoxes.

Theologians were disturbed by the calendar slippage, because the church sets the calendar date for Easter by identifying the first full moon after the Vernal Equinox. This is the same method the Jewish rabbis use to set the calendar date for the Passover feast.

Vatican Introduces New Calendar

When the Christians were breaking away from the Jewish-Aries traditions and moving further into the Piscean Age, they proclaimed, "We want our own new beginning or spring holiday."

The church clergy decided that the next Sunday after the Passover full moon would be designated as the Christian feast called *Easter*. When the Passover full moon falls on a Sunday, the Christians make the next Sunday after the full moon Easter. This ensures that Easter will never be celebrated on the first day of the Jewish Passover.

The church used the *Metonic cycle* of the moon to preset the calendar dates for Easter many years before the spring full moons occurred. The Metonic cycle is the same 18.6 year cycle of the moon caused by nutation.

When we look up the word "East" in a dictionary, we find that the strict definition is as follows: The place or direction where an observer on the equator sees the sun rise over the horizon on the day of an equinox. Hence we arrive at the word "Easter."

The problem Pope Gregory XIII and the church had was simple. The church was using the accurate solar beam to set Easter, but the Julian Calendar was regressing because of the precession of the equinoxes. Unless something was done, the calendar would keep slipping further back into *winter* and beyond.

Of course, that wouldn't do. After all, Easter symbolizes a new beginning or spring — not the return of winter.

Therefore, Pope Gregory decreed that everyone would go to bed on October 4, 1582, and when they awoke the next day it would be October 15, 1582. The Roman Catholic Church threw out ten days of history in order to set the calendar straight. This decree restored the Vernal Equinox to March 21.

After that, the Vatican astronomers invented the Gregorian Calendar that we still use today. They placed the leap years in February to assure the world that the calendar would show March 21 when the sunbeam hit the small circle on the marble floor in the Room of the Four Winds.

Gregorian Calendar

Thus, the two primary reasons we have leap years are to keep Easter in spring where it belongs and to keep our calendars in harmony with the astronomical cycles of the universe.

Most of the countries in Europe corrected their calendars in October with the Vatican, although the French hesitated briefly, then tossed out December 10, 1582, through December 19, 1582.

For nearly 170 years, the English would have no part of this until they realized what was happening and eliminated September 4, 1752, through September 13,

1752, to catch up. This was the same legislation that moved the first day of the New Year from spring to January 1 in the English calendar.

Even the Gregorian Calendar isn't perfect. It slips by one day in nearly 5,000 years. Around the year A.D. 6582, we will have to adjust our calendar by one day. Remember, the Egyptian calendar was slipping by one day every four years — even after it was adjusted by inserting five feast days at the close of each year.

Having been exposed to some of the ancient places of worship on the planet, we may be sensing how important the first day of spring was to many of our ancestors. They recognized how significant it is to adjust our calendars with the movements of the heavenly bodies.

Let us now move on to the next chapter where we will discover the first riddle of the Giza Sphinx as we continue glimpsing back through the ages.

5

The Egyptian Sphinx

In this chapter, we are going to disclose one of the more important riddles of the Giza Sphinx. In order to achieve this goal, we must continue looking back through the ages. When we stopped reviewing the bygone ages of our present Platonic year in Chapter 3, we had seen the Vernal-Equinox sun traverse Gemini, Taurus, Aries, and Pisces for around 2,150 years in each constellation.

Eight to ten thousand years ago the Vernal-Equinox sun was moving west through Cancer on the first day of spring. Even if we can read stone tablets or hieroglyphics, we can only surmise what was going on during this period of history, because most of the Western cultures start their records with Adam and Eve who are also known as the twins or Gemini.

Cancer is symbolized as a crab in today's world. In the most ancient Egyptian Zodiacs it is pictured as

Hermes, with the head of a hawk.

The very old Egyptian Zodiacs, from the temples of Denderah and Esneh, pictured Cancer as a *Scarabaeus* or Sacred Beetle. We also find an ancient Hindu Zodiac of 400 B.C. depicting the constellation of Cancer as a beetle.

The Scarab passes its early existence as a worm of the earth, and then it springs forth as a winged inhabitant of the heavens. It was the symbol of resurrection and fertility for the Egyptians. They depicted the beetle carrying the sun through the darkness of the night.

Before Cancer, ten to twelve thousand years ago, the sun was traversing west through Leo the Lion on the Spring Equinox. As a sacred animal, the lion is found in many legends, including the tales of Hercules who slaughtered the lion and wore its hide. It is also found over the gate of Mycenae and next to the throne in Pilos.

King of the Jungle

The lion has been used extensively as the symbol for supreme power, the kingdom, or ultimate justice. Even today, the constellation of Leo the Lion still represents power and is considered to be the most important *heraldic* constellation. We will shed more light on how the constellation of Leo the Lion heralds in the justice or balance of our coming times in another chapter.

Giza Sphinx

When we travel to Egypt, we find what must be the world's oldest man-made lion, and the only remaining wonder of *The Original Seven Wonders of the World* — the Great Pyramid of Giza with the Sphinx. The ancient Sphinx is facing East, waiting for the Sun God *Ra* to return.

Because the Spring-Equinox sun takes around 25,800 years to move in a westerly direction all the way around the Zodiac, the Sphinx has a long wait. Nevertheless, even though it is occasionally abused by man or nature, the Sphinx is weathering the ages especially well. Napoleon Bonaparte once blew its nose off with a few cannon balls. But what the heck! Nothing lasts forever.

The Sphinx has the body of a lion and the head of a human. Could it be Leo the Lion's body? We know, from astronomy, that the Spring-Equinox sun was traversing west through the constellation of Virgo, the Virgin, before it was in Leo the Lion. Why would the Egyptians place a picture of the Sphinx between Virgo and Leo in the ceiling of the Temple of Esneh's Portico?

They placed the Sphinx's head in Virgo the Virgin and its buttocks in Leo the Lion! Sphinx means to bind, to close, or to bring together, as the sphincter muscle (the lips) that binds the opening of our mouth closed. The Sphinx binds or closes the circle of the Zodiac between Virgo and Leo in this Platonic year, and it also marks the "New Years Day" of the great year.

However, the Egyptian Sphinx has the head of a man, so we know that the binding of Virgo and Leo is not the function of the Sphinx's most shrouded riddle. We will reveal this esoteric secret in another chapter of this book.

In the meantime, don't get bogged down with the vast amount of information being exposed in a short amount of time. Just keep moving — for most of us are not going to absorb in one reading the knowledge that took our ancestors many ages to record.

In most mythologies, the Virgin has a child. In Egypt the child is Horus, in Greece the child is Christos, and in Persia the child is Ihesu. Each of the twelve major constellations has three minor constellations that the astrologers and the astronomers use to map the stars of the heavens into distinct groups. The first sub-constellation of Virgo in ancient Zodiacs was *Coma*, the desired or longed-for child.

Virgin and Child

At some point in history, Berenice, the wife of the Egyptian king Euergetes, had her wig stolen from the Temple of Venus. To appease poor Berenice, Connon, an astronomer from Alexandria (283-222 B.C.), initiated a fairy tale. He said that Jupiter had taken her hair and made it into a constellation.

Consequently, the Virgin's child is now called *Berenice's Hair,* not Coma, by present day astronomers and astrologers. Shakespeare reminded us of the truth in *Titus Andronicus* (Act IV, Scene 3) when he spoke of shooting the arrow to the good boy in Virgo's lap.

Many scholars reaffirm the connection between our religious stories and the constellations of the heavens when they state that the *Star of Bethlehem* first appeared in the constellation of Coma, the Virgin's child.

If you are interested in the origins of star names and constellations, find a copy of *Glory of the Stars* by E. Raymond Capt.

Everything we have been talking about so far has to do with the position of our sun in the Zodiac on successive Vernal Equinoxes. Let us take a quick look at how the sun travels through the twelve star constellations during the rest of the year, so thereafter we may discover the origin of an ancient religious allegory.

In the yearly cycle of our Earth, we notice the sun moving in the opposite direction of the sun's precession in the Platonic year. In one year, our solar sun moves through a different constellation each month.

At this time in history, most of us are still calling Aries the First Sign of the Zodiac. Therefore, according to the astrologers, from March 21 (the first day of spring) to April 20 the sun is in Aries, then April 21 to

May 20 the sun is in Taurus, May 21 to June 20 the sun is in Gemini, et cetera.

Instead of starting with Aries as the first sun sign of the Zodiac for our yearly cycle, move the point of origin back to the center of the Sphinx, which binds Virgo and Leo. This was the location of the Vernal-Equinox sun in the Zodiac on March 21 at the start of our present Platonic year nearly 13,000 years ago.

Now let us view the mythological story of the Virgin to the final kingdom as the ancient sphinx builders must have seen it, when they observed the sun traveling each month through the twelve constellations of the Zodiac.

Sphinx Binds Virgo & Leo

They would have viewed the sun leave the head of the Sphinx on the first day of their New Year, which occurred on March 21, and they would have recorded that it took one month to move through Virgo with her child Coma. Then the sun would have traversed Libra with the Southern Cross from April 21 to May 20.

The sun would have continued moving day by day via the rest of the twelve constellations of the Zodiac. At the end of one regular year, our sun would have ended up midway between Virgo and Leo, which the Egyptians represented as the middle of the Sphinx.

In other words, the sun starts its yearly rounds at the Virgin with her child, and it ends up in the Final Kingdom after passing through the rump of the Sphinx — which represents Leo the Lion, or the kingdom.

When we use the symbol of the Sphinx as a marker for our Earth year, we discover the ancient Christian story of the *Virgin to the Final Kingdom* marked in stone. I am not going to touch that with a ten foot pole other than to say, if I teach you to tie a knot before we have a break in our relationship, you will still use the knot I taught you because — it works.

In the upcoming chapter, we are going to divulge some more revealing information that may cause us to revel as we discover our present position in this Platonic year. Let's explore onward.

6

The Ages of Our World

We can use the Giza Sphinx, one of the oldest markers on the planet Earth, to locate our present position in this Platonic year. Starting our measure from the center of the Sphinx, we know the Vernal-Equinox sun traveled west through Leo the Lion for a little over two thousand years. That would be the First Age of the world, or the Age of Leo.

The sun continued traversing through the constellation of Cancer for another two thousand plus years. This would be the Second Age of the world in our present great year.

The Spring-Equinox sun moved west through Gemini for an additional 2,150 years. That is the Third Age of this Platonic year. The spring sun crossed through Taurus the Bull for the next few thousand years. This was known as the Fourth Age or the Age of Taurus.

The sun's apparent movement through the Zodiac continued as the spring equinoctial point moved west through Aries the Ram, 4,000 to 6,000 years ago. If you're still counting with me, this period of time was the Fifth Age of the world.

For the last two thousand plus years, the sun has been moving west in Pisces the Fish. This is the *Sixth Age* of the world — the Piscean Age in our current Platonic year.

Using the Sphinx as a marker for the start of this Platonic year, it indicates that we are now at or very near the halfway point in this cycle. Six is halfway around the twelve constellations of the Zodiac.

Vatican Proclaims Pisces the Sixth Age

Even the Roman Catholic Church informs us that it was the Sixth Age of the world when Jesus, the fisherman of souls, was born. Listen with the Pope every Christmas Eve as a member of the clergy reads the beloved Martyrologier or Calends on a live broadcast of Midnight Mass from the Vatican in Rome.

The Calends, or calendar, reads in part, "In the time of the 194th Olympiad; in the year 752 after the foundation of Rome; in the 42nd year of the Empire of Octavian Augustus Caesar; while peace reigned in all the earth; in the Sixth Age of the world; Jesus Christ, . . . was born."

The Sixth Age of the world in this Platonic year is the *Piscean Age*. As we stated earlier in this work, the Piscean fish is one the most common Christian symbols. Check a few car bumper stickers if you are not sure about this statement.

The most important star in today's heavens had the Arabic name *Al Ruccaba*, which means the *turned* or *ridden on*. We all know this star as Polaris, our North Pole Star. Why did the ancient Semitic astronomers call Al Ruccaba the "Turning Point Star" 7,000 years before it became our North Pole Star in this Platonic year? Does this mean that the end of the Sixth Age is the *turning point* in the 25,800 year cycle?

Using 10 percent or less of my brain power, I don't profess to know the answers. I am only placing these ideas and questions on the table for all of us to sift through, and for us to integrate what is true into our own lives and toss out what is false.

For those of us who are "into" Plato's history of the sinking of Atlantis, he places the sinking around twelve to thirteen thousand years ago. In his famous book *The Lost Continent of Mu,* James Churchward places the sinking of Atlantis, Lemuria, and Mu between twelve and thirteen thousand years ago. Notice that this is halfway back in our present Platonic year.

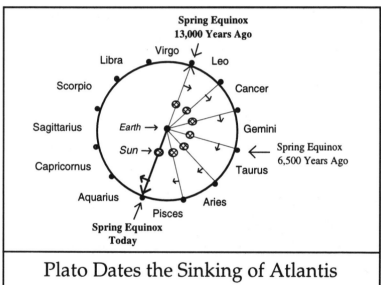

Plato Dates the Sinking of Atlantis

Now we can talk about the prophecies of Edgar Cayce, Nostradamus, the American Indians, Revelations, and all the other predictions which point to this approaching time as a period of great changes for the planet Earth.

When we think of cycles, we can think of going and coming, falling and rising, getting lost and being found, or veiling and unveiling. At the end of the Sixth

Age, we may be looking for comings, be far from the garden, nearly out of the light, and rather lost, using only 10 percent of our brain's potential.

As a piece of music has bars between the measures, and as a play has veils between the acts, we may be doing measures of time, or veiling and unveiling, in the cycles of Platonic years. Unfortunately, we have no records of earlier Platonic years to compare ourselves to. The only remains that we have been able to discover are a lot of old bones.

"Who Needs Changes?"

In summing up what information we have covered so far, I would say that we are near or at the end of an age, we are approaching the half-way turning point in our present Platonic year, and we can expect some very big changes.

Relax! The planet is at least four billion years old. The dinosaurs have been extinct for nearly 65 million years. We have spiraled through 39 Platonic years in just the last million years. This is not the end of the world; in fact, everything is progressing as it is written.

I would say, though, that this is a time of *revelations*. It is time to *reveal* the truth. It is also a time to *revel*, which means a time for *celebrating, merrymaking*, and *festivities*. Everything is happening in perfect harmony with the astronomical cycles of our universe. The razing of the falling age will give way to the spring of a new one.

Let us move with the flow, and see what the four ancient genies, who are coming up on our time machine's computer, are going to disclose to us in the following chapter.

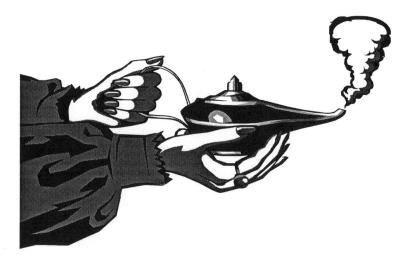

7

The Four Genii

In this chapter we are going to learn about the four heads of the beast, or the Four Genii as they are called in some of our more ancient legends. Let us begin by looking at the word "genii," which is the plural form of the word "genius."

One could define genius as a person of phenomenal and original powers or as the guardian spirit of a person. A genius is higher and more spontaneous than talent, less dependent than others on instruction, and not always amenable to training. Genii can have an extraordinary influence over another being or humanity in general.

The Four Genii are found in many legends and mythologies of the original creation. The most ancient ones called them *Pillars of Heaven* or *Pillars of Him who Dwells in the Heavens.* The heavens were sustained by four pillars, and each pillar had one of the Four Genii as a keeper to take charge of it. The Four Genii are sometimes represented as the four cardinal points of a cross in a square or circle. We will also discover them in another chapter as the four corner sockets of the Great Pyramid of Giza.

The Maya called them *Kan Bacab* (yellow, and placed in the East), *Chac Bacab* (red, and placed in the West), *Zac Bacab* (white, and placed in the North), and *Ek Bacab* (black, and placed in the South).

To the Chaldeans they were the protecting Genii of the human race: *Sed-Alap* or *Kirub*, a bull with a human face; *Lamas* or *Nigal*, a lion with a man's head; *Ustar,* a human; and *Nattig,* an eagle with a human face.

Confucius Says —"Remember the Four Genii"

We can also find the Four Genii in Chinese and Hindu mythologies. If you are interested in this subject, secure a copy of *The Lost Continent of Mu* by Colonel James Churchward, and you won't be disappointed.

The Jewish populace will come across the Four Genii in the Old Testament under Ezekiel 1:10: *As for the likeness of their faces, the cherubims, they had a face of a man; and they four had the face of a lion on the right side; and they four had the face of an ox on the left side; they four had also the face of an eagle.*

The Christians call them the four *heads of the beast*, the four *living creatures,* or the four *cherubim.* We can read about them in the New Testament under Revelations 4:6-7: *The floor around the throne was like a sea of glass that was crystal-clear. At the very center, around the throne itself, stood four living creatures covered with eyes front and back. The first creature resembled a lion, the second an ox, the third had the face of a man, while the fourth looked like an eagle in flight.*

All through Egyptian antiquities and artifacts we see the Four Genii depicted as the four minor sphinxes. We find this depiction, for example, in much of the Egyptian or English documentation of the Giza Pyramid, and of other Egyptian temples — one a sphinx with a lion's head, one with a bull's head, another with an eagle's head, and the last one with a human's head.

The Four Genii are called *Kerubim* in the Thoth Tarot Deck. They are placed in the four corners of Trump Card V (The Hierophant), Trump Card VI (The Lovers), Trump Card XXI (The Universe). We can also find them illustrated in many other cards together or separately.

They are also pictured as the four minor Egyptian sphinxes on Trump Card VII (The Chariot). They are pulling the chariot with a man whose only function is to bear the Holy Grail. He is throned in the chariot rather than conducting it, because the whole system of progression is perfectly balanced and proceeding in a natural flow.

The tarot is an illustrated model of the forces of nature as conceived by the ancients. *Rota* is a wheel. Hence we get the word *tarota* or in modern times *tarot*. The solar system, with the planets revolving around the solar sun, is not a sphere. It is a *wheel*. The planet's orbits are elliptical. The ancients paid very close attention to the rim or belt of this wheel, and they called it the *Zodiac*.

"Going to Make a Fortune"

Even the origin of our modern playing cards can be historically traced to the four suits of the tarot cards. Don't let any misuse of the tarot deck detract you from the ancient origins and knowledge contained in pictorial form within them. For more information refer to *The Book of Thoth* by Aleister Crowley.

Everything we have been talking about in all these chapters has been based on the Spring Equinox which occurs on March 21. What do we know about the Autumnal Equinox, on or near September 22, when the sun's plane crosses the equator heading south towards the Tropic of Capricorn? Almost everything we have said about the Vernal Equinox holds true for the Autumnal Equinox, except that the Fall-Equinox sun crosses on the opposite side of the celestial equator.

The Vernal Equinox is going into Aquarius, the *Man,* at this time in the Platonic year, and the Autumnal Equinox is just dawning into Leo, the *Lion,* for the next 2,150 years. That accounts for two heads of those winged beasts or cherubim if I am counting right.

"Genii Soup"

If I thought I could make this chapter any easier for us to digest by eating those two winged monsters and having the other two for dessert when they finish stewing in my brain, I would do so (even though I am a total vegetarian). It would be worth it just to free the universe for all time of these spiraling monsters. Next time we should make them Mickey, Minnie, Donald, and Goofy. It's much easier to comprehend these four genii.

Let us make a model to see if we can locate and understand the two missing Genii. Picture a right angle cross with four arms of equal length. Place the Autumnal Equinox and Leo the Lion at the end of the top arm. Put the Spring Equinox and Aquarius the Man on the bottom arm of the cross on the same line as Leo the Lion.

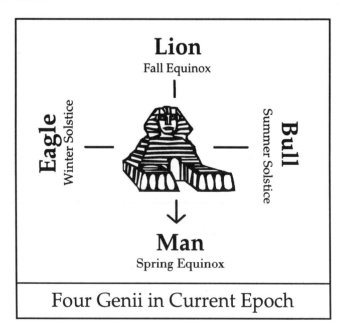

Lion
Fall Equinox

Eagle
Winter Solstice

Bull
Summer Solstice

Man
Spring Equinox

Four Genii in Current Epoch

Now take the Sphinx, that runs around binding things together, and skewer it on the vertical beam of the cross between Aquarius and Leo. Calm Down! We're using imaginary lines, so it doesn't hurt. Now that we all have the Sphinx on the vertical beam of the cross binding the Man and the Lion, we are getting our first glimpse of the male aspect of the hermaphroditic Sphinx.

In due time, we will meet the Sphinx and a few of its mythological friends on our journey to the twilight zone. They will unite to reveal their hidden-timely symbol, but, as you can plainly see, I don't mind lifting a few cow patties to expose some clues on the way.

Let us remove the Sphinx from our imaginary cross and return it to the Zodiac to bind Virgo, the Virgin, and Leo, the Lion. Now the Sphinx has its feminine face or aspect again.

Place the Summer Solstice of June 21 on the right arm of the cross. It is just Dawning into Taurus, the *Bull*, at this time in the Platonic year. Put that Bull there, over the Summer Solstice. The Summer Solstice will take the next 2,150 years to travel west through the constellation of Taurus.

Let's place the Winter Solstice on the left arm of the cross, and then we can go find that Eagle who cohabits with a Scorpion. Yes, they dwell in the constellation of Scorpio, which Abraham of Biblical fame always called the *Eagle*. Put that Eagle on the left end of the cross.

If we check the heavens on December 21, we will find the Winter-Solstice sun is just dawning into Scorpio, and it will be traversing that constellation for the next 2,150 years.

Now we can observe how the Four Genii look when the cross lines up with them at this time in the Platonic year. Let us take the four Genii off the cross and put them into the wheel of the Zodiac where they belong. We will leave the Spring and Autumnal Equinoxes, along with the Summer and Winter Solstices, attached to the ends of the cross.

Now put the cross in the middle of the Zodiac and spin it. Don't hold your breath! The cross is going to take 25,800 years to make one revolution. Notice! We have the ancient and universal symbol for the planet Earth — a cross in a circle.

Let me show you a trick. Turn the cross to put the Vernal Equinox in Aries where it was 2,000 to 4,000 years ago. Now check the right arm of the cross where the Summer Solstice is attached. If all is going well, it should be in the constellation of Cancer.

This gives us the Tropic of Cancer on every map and globe. Check the location of the Winter Solstice.

That's right! It is in the Tropic of Capricorn that is also depicted on our maps and globes. That was our position in this great year 2,000 to 4,000 years ago.

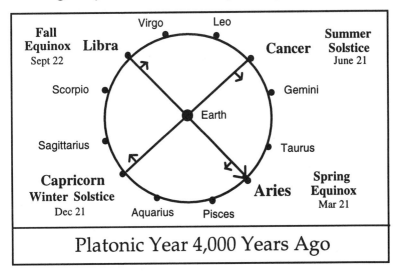

Fall Equinox Libra Sept 22 · Virgo · Leo · Cancer · Summer Solstice June 21 · Scorpio · Gemini · Earth · Sagittarius · Taurus · Capricorn Winter Solstice Dec 21 · Aquarius · Pisces · Aries · Spring Equinox Mar 21

Platonic Year 4,000 Years Ago

Turn the Vernal Equinox to the Sixth Age of the world or the Piscean Age. That is where the first day of spring has been for the last 2,000 years. We have the Tropic of Gemini replacing the Tropic of Cancer on the Summer Solstice. We also find the Winter Solstice on the Tropic of Sagittarius instead of the Tropic of Capricorn.

The map and globe makers must have fallen asleep with the astrologers for the last 2,000-plus years! It is beginning to look as if they may have their work cut out for them. Using 10 percent of our brain's potential at the end of the Sixth Age, maybe we are all a little behind the times.

One of the purposes of this book is to remind the map makers and the astrologers of their responsibility to rectify the names of the solstices and the equinoxes on our charts, maps, and globes. When we finish reading this book and you fully comprehend the secrets being revealed to you, I hope that you will support me when I request that we upgrade our maps and charts.

Let us keep turning the cross and put the first day of Spring at the dawning of Aquarius, where we are at this time in the Platonic year. Yes! Our Four Genii are lining up again.

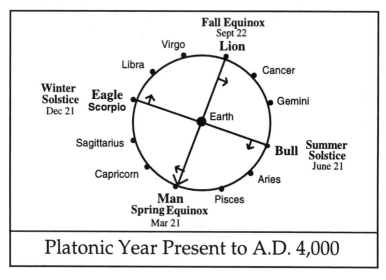

Platonic Year Present to A.D. 4,000

Our Summer Solstice is in Taurus, so we can change the Tropic of Cancer on our maps and globes to the Tropic of Taurus. Ah, the Winter Solstice is in Scorpio, so the Tropic of Capricorn needs to be renamed the Tropic of Scorpio.

70

The Autumnal Equinox is in Leo the Lion, the Vernal Equinox is in Aquarius the Man, the Summer Solstice is in Taurus the Bull, and the Winter Solstice is in Scorpio with the Eagle.

Spring is going into the Man and Fall is going into the Lion during this era in the Platonic year. I believe, as we enter this major turning point, we will start to remember who we are and from whence we sprang. Man's lower-animalistic essence begins to fall into the beastly lion as his spiritual being re-emerges.

Now take the cross and spin it 180 degrees. This puts Spring into the beast and Fall into the Man. This is 13,000 years ago when Atlantis, Lemuria, and Mu supposedly sank.

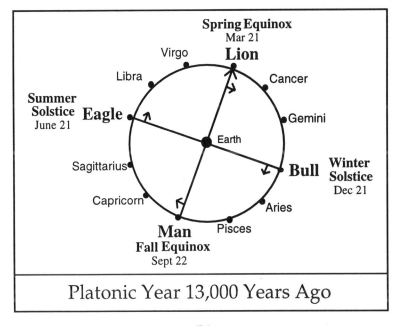

Platonic Year 13,000 Years Ago

This era in the Platonic year can be interpreted in some of the creation stories as the fall of man into the beast or the fall from the garden. This was the time when mankind's spring was cut short because he was bullheaded enough to be tricked and stung by the scorpion. Man was expelled from the garden and cast into the darkness of the lion's jungle.

Genesis 3:24 says: *The cherubim, with wings like an eagle, were stationed with fiery revolving swords to guard the way to the tree of life.*

Has anybody heard this allegory before? If this information is ringing a bell and you are still interested in un-weaving some more fascinating material, take a deep breath, close your eyes, and let what we are learning sink in. When you're ready, spin into the spelling class coming up in the next chapter, and we will have some more fun playing school.

8

The Spell of the Universe

N ow that we have explored some of the physical aspects of the Platonic year, we are going to balance ourselves by devoting the next two chapters to the philosophical dimensions of this great year. Even though some of the inferences I make only work in English, you should be able to translate the overall concept into any language.

In this chapter we are going to unravel some of the *spells* that were woven into many of our myths, and we are going to begin by taking a closer look at *words* and a few of the ways they can be used to influence us.

Picture me talking to you in person rather than through this writing. I would be speaking to you in a fairly monotone voice. You could say to me, "Stop talking and open up your mouth as wide as you can, but keep the sound coming out." If I keep my mouth wide open with my tongue out of the way, *Ah* is the only sound that I can produce.

You can use the sound from a piano or other musical instrument to find out what note dominates the limited range on which I speak to you. In the middle of a sentence, have me switch from talking to producing a steady *Ah* sound. Using the different pitches of the musical instrument as a gauge, check what pitch I have been babbling on.

When we go to a medical center for a physical, the physician says: "Open your mouth and say *'Ah'* while I check you out." All spoken words have their roots in the sound of *Ah*.

Music is different! We stop in the middle of a sentence and open up our mouths wide so we are creating a monotone. When we keep our mouths open, we can change the note or pitch we are *Ah*-ing on. Go up and down the music scales like a singer who is exercising her voice.

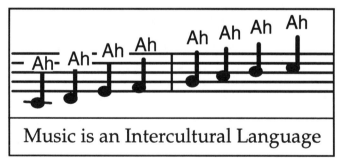

Music is an Intercultural Language

I can't write the sound the singer is making using the words of this book, but I can use music notation to give you an approximation of how to reproduce it.

If we create something sad with music, a lot of people around the world will cry. Should we play something scary, such as war drumming in a jungle, many people will hide. When we perform something spiritual in music, a few people might look up into the heavens, while others may look at a sacred rock, cross, icon, or whatever symbol their culture deems special.

"Get My Message?"

When we use music as the medium, many of the diverse inhabitants on the planet will perceive the emotional communication that the musician is expressing. We can also ornament a musical composition using words, just as we enhance our Christmas trees with decorations.

There are many levels of communication beyond music that we can use. Mathematics, body language, eye contact, and touch are just a few examples of these levels. It should be obvious, therefore, that words can be very powerful, but they are still one of the lower forms of communication.

We can use the medium of words to *cast spells* or charm people. On the power of suggestion, people heal themselves with placebo pills occasionally. We can be hypnotized and told that we are being bitten on the arm by a mosquito; the body will produce a bump.

A speech writer writes a good speech, and we are spellbound by the discourse. We can also be mesmerized by a good book. In fact, we even ask our kids if they passed their *spelling* class.

Spell Caster

Now that we all know what level of communication words are on, I should be able to narrate a mythological story to allude to something beyond the words, and no reasonable being will be offended that I didn't use his or her favorite utterance. We are now going to use the powerful medium of words to dispel some of the hypnotic myths that are disabling the masses.

Most of these spells were cast into writing during the Age of Taurus, 4,000 to 6,000 years ago. Maybe this explains why some of us run around the planet babbling that this folklore or that legend is all B.S.

The myths that many of us were taught from birth were cast in a fairly mediocre form of communication that uses the spell of words. Using the very words these myths were cast in, we will break their power over us so that we can interpret them with a bird's-eye view.

Eventually, each of us should be deprogrammed enough to soar into the heavens on our own, but in the meantime, we should not be fighting wars over different mythological stories.

You might think I was unenlightened should I say, "If you profess any other fable than 'Cinderella,' you will be severely punished for eternity. I don't want to hear anything about Snow White or King Arthur and the Knights of the Round Table. I will only accept the story of 'Cinderella' as the true word."

How foolish! All of these fairy tales are reducible to *Ah*. Now that we are clear about this, I am going to express *my th*ing, myth, or belief as an allegory.

Let each of us think about the word we use for the whole universe. Pick a word or sound that includes everything in creation, as well as the force or power that created it. Some people use the sound or word *Ah, Om, Aum, God*, or *Allah* just to mention a few.

I am going to use the word *Oneness* or *Whole*. Remember, it is just a word representing something beyond the words. This is one of the reasons the great sages always spoke in parables, mythology stories, folklore, or legends about something that cannot be expressed within the confines of words.

The Oneness or the Whole says to Itself: I am everything! I am God! I am It! I am the point or a perfect circle! God I am bored! I am so tired of playing with Myself. This is ridiculous. I am tired of being all one or alone.

"Boring"

Notice that "all one" and "alone" are essentially the same. If one is all one, then one must be alone. Are we sensing the predicament of the One Who Causes?

Being absolutely bored, the Oneness comes up with a bright idea. Why! I'll just split into two. This would be the same way we split into two teams to play football, chess, or checkers. The Perfect Circle, God, or the Whole gets imaginative, and It splits *in two* or *in-to* creation.

In-Divided-Dual or an Individual

Once the Oneness or God splits into the two U's (You & You, Us or We), what is a game the universe can play? "Hide and Seek" of course! God can hide from Itself, and spend Its Being trying to find Itself. Give me space to find myself! I have been found! I found it! Most of us know that lost and found departments are normally found together.

A Double of You or A Double U

The game of the universe is Hide and Seek. Dismember to separate. Re-member is to put it back together again, or to remember something we have forgotten. Every baby knows this intuitively, until we teach it to babble or <u>Babylon</u> (baby-on) in words.

Babylon was the language center in ancient times. The name itself means to confound, and it refers to the confusion of tongues at the tower of Babel. Genesis 11:5-9 says *the Lord came down to see the city and the tower that the men had built. He realized that they were all one people who spoke the same language, and if they were already building the tower, nothing would stop them from doing whatever they presumed later. So the Lord confused their language and spread them all over the world.*

Even the word "charmer" is understood by some as babbler in Eccles. 10:11, and Paul is called a "babbler" in Acts 17:18. Accordingly, babies babble before learning one or more languages. In the meantime, they love to play "Peek a Boo." Make it gone! Make it come back! Turn on the Light. Turn off the Light. *Cycles!*

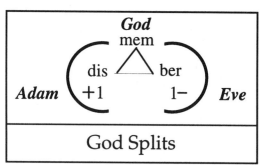

Actually the original split of the Whole is not just dual, or two. When it comes to you and I, we are part of a mystical triangle with God as cosmic consciousness or *mem*ory. You and I are left in duality, at the base of the triangle, trying to balance, re*mem*ber or recollect with God who is depicted as the third point of that triangle.

As we traversed the past few Ages of this Platonic year, the ultimate realization, in philosophy, was "I Am." Hence, we say, "You Are." The truth of our one-ness, even in duality, was degraded into the dark concept of one side wins over the other. We carried this thinking to the point of man over woman, day over night, kingdoms over populace, dictators over masses, or master gurus over slave followers.

Coming around the halfway point of this great year, we are noticing a natural change taking place in the words we are using to communicate. "We are" is replacing "I am" at the end of the Sixth Age. Jesus said, *"When Two or More are Gathered in My Name, I Am Present."* Two or more is a "we." In today's world or philosophies, the correct declaration is "We are."

"We are Going to Eat."

Even the top executives in the sales industry will inform us that it is better to say to the customer: "We can deliver this by Friday." The word "we" includes every being involved in the manufacture of this product and all the creators of methods used to deliver it to you.

We observe the foreshadowing change of consciousness in the United States Constitution when it starts out with these words, *"We the people, in order to form a more perfect union."* Notice the word *union*. It can be separated into *uni* plus *one*. U N I can also be written as you and I are one.

Now that we are beginning to comprehend the magic of words and see that the fundamental game of the universe is Hide and Seek, we are going to shed some light on the "hide" stage of the game as we proceed to unravel the secrets of the Sphinx.

9

Enlightenment One

Once we ascertain that the game of the universe is Hide and Seek, we could ask ourselves: "How does the Oneness hide from Itself?" In this chapter, we are going to explore the "hide" stage of the game and the ways that the symbols of our impending and departing ages indicate our position in this game.

We already know that the first split is one to one, eye to eye, or point to point. We might further observe that it takes two points connected with a line to construct the numeral for the number one. In other words, it takes two to make a whole.

In fact, we can only look into one set of eyes at a time, and, when we do, we start to experience things differently as the two energies start to harmonize as one. Most people glance away to break the connection, as they do not understand what is taking place. Some blind people keenly sense this unity on a conscious level that most of us with sight do not comprehend.

Looking at the original split of the Creator in math or electrical terminology, we see that creation first divides into one positive and one negative. In electricity, one volt of polarity has less attraction than a small flashlight battery with 1.5 volts potential. There would be a minute spark if we caused a momentary short between the poles, and nothing happens when we touch both sides with our fingertips.

It only takes a small insulator to hold the two forces apart, even though they want to spring back together. If we put them very close to one another, they will leap back together, because they are seeking unity the same as U N I are pursuing reunion.

We wouldn't be reading this chapter right now if we weren't questing for unity. OK! Maybe it was the only book left at the hair salon, as everyone else grasped the righteous revelations and left this for you. It has been said that there are no accidents in the universe, but what do I know of these coincidences? Not very much, so let us continue exploring our electrical model of God split into the opposite poles or the duality of our universe.

When we connect an incandescent lamp between electrical polarities, the electrons run through the light bulb trying to get back together. As the tiny filament narrows the only path the electrons can use inside the bulb, they produce heat and light as they push their way through the restricted path.

Incandescent Lamp

This is what electricity is all about. The light bulb or electrical appliance will not work unless we have both the negative and positive. If all the electrons get back together, we will end up with nothing (no thing) or a dead battery.

Let us try to make one side win over the other by increasing the positive to 120 plus. OOPS! What's this? The opposite side increased to 120 negative. We didn't want this! We wanted the positive to be triumphant, and look what happened! They balanced themselves, and we ended up with the plus mutually attracted to the opposite minus.

Ah! Picture two things tied together with a rubber band. The more we pull them apart the more they want to come together. We will need a larger insulator to keep them apart. We use much thicker rubber or insulation on our electric-television cords than we need for battery-operated toys.

Let us get more intense and try harder to make the positive win. We will increase the positive to 220 plus. Darn it! The opposite side increased to 220 negative. We will have to purchase a heavy duty wire with much more insulation to keep these two apart if we are going to run our electric range.

For those of you on the dark side, let us try to make the negative force prevail by increasing it to 66,000 minus. We will do those positives in, right here and now. What! Those *#^*&%^ pluses increased to 66,000 positive!

Now we have to buy a power pole with a six foot glass insulator to keep these two apart. If they get anywhere near each other, the spark they create jumping back together could set the whole neighborhood on fire.

As we increase the positive, we create more devils to combat. When we produce more negative, we create more good to contest. They are always found together, and they want to get back together. Having been stretched so far apart, they lose sight of each other, and they forget the reality that they are inseparably tied together.

The more we stretch them apart, the more they are attracted to one another. It will take a much thicker veil or insulator to keep them from flying back together. Should we remove the insulator, or velum, suddenly with an enormous amount of attraction between them, the spark would be intense.

"OOPS!"

In the game of Hide and Seek, the "hide" stage is in full manifestation once we believe that one side ought to win over the other. The harder we try to make one side victorious over the other, the more lost, or insulated from reality, we become. The insulator is the veil that allows some of us to believe this sorcery.

The concept that good wins over evil was initiated by primitive cultures who based this battle on the alternation of day and night. As we begin this era of Revelations, we are awakening to comprehend the truth — that the opposites are inseparable.

You wouldn't let me come to your room tonight and say, "Day wins over night! Day wins over night! Don't go to sleep! Day wins over night!" After spending the day reading a book like this, you would pick up the lamp and say, "You get out of here right now! I'll see you in the morning. I am just going to sleep for a little while."

We will let an unaware doctor take the Hippocratic Oath that life wins over death. An elderly person says; "Doctor I am not hungry. I just want to fast for a few days." The unaware doctor starts declaring, "Life wins over death! Life wins over death! I am going to tie you down and force-feed you with these tubes up your nose."

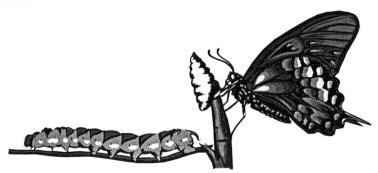

"Do I Have a Choice in this Matter?"

The old person explains, "Doctor, I am seeing a higher light. I've already done all the things you are just discovering and finding interesting. I am just a caterpillar metamorphosing into a butterfly."

The unaware doctor replies, "No way! I have taken an oath to keep you alive. I am going to dispel any ideas you have of transcending the bounds of this planet and force you to crawl as a caterpillar on the face of this Earth, even if I have to go against your wishes and tie you down with happy pills or straps." Luckily, there are many conscious and qualified physicians at our beckoning, although much of our antiquated legislation ties all of our hands severely.

"Wise Up"

Remember to treat our sick and elderly, who are attempting to make a smooth transition, the way you would want to be treated if you were in their shoes. What we teach our kids to be the correct way of handling death is the way they will respond to the situation when we are ready to pass over.

What we put out is what comes back. Let us start thinking about our future predicament right here and now. Do you want that tube up your nose when you say no?

If a person says, "Save Me! Save Me!" then, as long as both parties agree, *Go for it.* Do whatever you want! Have a ball or half brain if you please. All we ask is that our legislators and medical personnel respect our wishes should we choose to make a smooth transition through the veil. Life and death go together. "Ashes to ashes and dust to dust." Do we have a problem with this basic truth?

We wouldn't say the top of the mountain wins over its base. Most of us know that the higher up the mountain we go, the deeper the valley becomes. We wouldn't say hot water prevails over cold water, because we are smart enough to realize that the hotter the hot feels, the colder the cold feels. If we put the two together, they would neutralize each other.

We keep them in containers with insulation or a velum between them to maintain their different temperatures. *Velation* is the forming of a velum or partition, and *revelation* is removing that partition or veil and seeing the truth or awakening.

Why would anyone believe his right hand wins over his left? Try making your right hand defeat the left one. No! Hit that left hand harder! Wait a minute! Let me try what I asked you to do. God that hurt! I hurt myself, because it is painful to try to force one side to triumph over the other. Being out of harmony with the truth causes pain or dis-ease!

The hide stage of the game is the belief that good wins over evil. The more we stretch them apart, the more they want to go back together and the more insulated we are from the truth.

"You Tricky Devil"

When we spell the word *live* backwards, we produce the word *evil*. Try spelling the word *lived* backwards. How about that for the riddle of words and spelling! Lived spelled backwards is the word *devil*. Please don't spin this book or any sacred publication backwards. Remember, I am revealing this with love, because the hour is near for a lot of us to perceive the truth.

Let us pretend that positive can conquer negative for a moment or two. We are going through this life thinking good vanquishes evil. We are praying that our right hands are up at the moment of our deaths, not our left ones. For us, life is a *test*.

Does anybody remember what a final exam was like on Friday? God! When can we get this quiz over with so we can play on Saturday? Picture your whole life as a final test.

We are going through life having good and bad thoughts. All we want to do is get this burdensome test over with so we can go play with the Oneness in heaven. Our whole life is one oppressive exam. Any sensible being would want to get the test over with so we can play. Even ending the test with a bullet to the head is cheating, so we do it slowly by over-indulgence of foods, et cetera — that way, it won't look like suicide.

Let us pretend we all died together. I am not against pretending this, because anyone who made it to this sentence is all right with me. We are all seekers of truth on the path. Smile and give yourself credit. Everything happens for a reason. Also, there is nothing new under the sun — only repackaging.

Okay! Back to pretending we just died together. As luck would have it, we all made it to heaven forever and ever. Now twenty billion, million, trillion, zillion years have passed, and we have just started eternity. We finally look over at God and say, "I passed your silly test on Earth. Now can we play?"

God replies, "Oh! You want to play. How would you like me to image (created in my image or imagination) planet Earth again as I did the first time?"

"Not Earth Again"

We protest, "No way! You had us down there on Earth thinking one side wins over the other. The more we tried to make one side triumph, the more insulated from the truth we became."

God says, "Well! You used to like to buy tickets to fun houses and get caught in a maze. ('Amazing Grace' is the light or knowledge to find our way out of the fun house.) You used to like scary movies to frighten or lose yourself. Do you want to play planet Earth again, or shall we create a new game?"

We might want to play planet Earth one more time after all those years have passed. Is this what reincarnation is all about? Surprise! It may be time to accept the fact that we bought the ticket to this fun house. We *agreed* to play Hide and Seek. God split into duality, and the game started.

Once we change the word-spell from "Life is a test" to "Life is a puzzle or a fun house," everything changes. It is a much lighter view to see life as a fun house rather than a final exam. The first step in getting *enlightened* is to change our viewpoint from a burdensome test to an amusing puzzle.

If the original incantations were cast in words, then we must use these same words to undo the hex. After that, we can throw the words away or charm a new spell. This is a spelling class called "Enlightenment One."

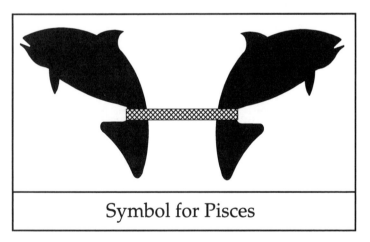

Symbol for Pisces

The Piscean symbol for the last 2,000 years depicts our spiritual predicament. It is two fish, banded together by their tails, trying to swim apart. Some of us carried this belief to the point of putting one fish on the car bumper and saying we must get rid of the other fish at all cost.

This point of view is the most lost stage of the game of Hide and Seek, but it is *necessary* to play. The end of the Piscean Age is the furthest from the Garden or the most lost moment before the halfway turning point in a Platonic year.

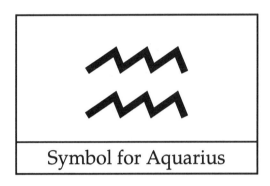

Symbol for Aquarius

Coming through the turn, we will find ourselves in the Seventh Age or the Age of Aquarius. The symbol for this age is depicted as two jagged lines that could fit together. This symbol may indicate that it is time to remember what has been dismembered or separated. At this juncture in the Platonic year, mankind peeks through the veil or insulator and sees that the opposites are connected.

This is a time of *atonement* or at-one-ment. We look down at our two hands and comprehend that they are connected. We catch the joke of the universe. We don't get upset about the ideologies of the last two thousand years or the earlier parts of our lives. We laugh at the fact that the joke was on us.

Knowing math and electricity, how could I have been so ignorant of the truth that I was snared into this word prank? Once we grasp the joke or solve the riddle of the puzzle, we can't go back. It is that simple! We've been had! We scared the britches off us! Peek a Boo! We see us!

"Help!"

But don't think the carnival is over yet. Any good amusement may have a major thrill or rush near the end of the ride. Enjoy it, knowing that everything is progressing as intended. See the humor in the paradoxical situations in which we find ourselves.

The *Book of Revelations* predicts that the whole planet will get ugly at this time in the Platonic year. That's why we should be reveling and celebrating joyously. The Bible is right on the mark! Our interpretation is off when we think that anything is happening outside the ultimate plan or desire of the Creator!

It is also okay to "Boo" the villains in God's play. Just do it with love. The only rule is: "What we put out comes back. We reap what we sow." Try to remember that everything is going as planned, and that we need only to align ourselves with that plan.

The most adventurous souls on the planet are those who still think one side wins over the other even while they say that God is everything. They are the deepest into the fun house or maze.

Everyone Gets Out — "Eventually"

Picture yourself as having saved enough money to purchase a ticket to the haunted-fun house at the carnival Saturday night. I walk into the maze and say to you, "What are you doing looking into that mirror? The way out is over here." Most likely, you're going to be upset with me for curtailing your amusement.

Imagine that you are entertaining yourself with a puzzle, and I saunter by and reveal the intricacies of the riddle before you have had a chance to solve it. Are you going to feel enchanted with me, or will you think I've interfered in your pleasure?

Don't try to awaken someone who is not ready to come out of the fun house. What are a few years in the maze called planet Earth in comparison to a few billion years of eternity? Appreciate where we are. History has shown that it has been unkind to those who try to rush it.

In fact, "rushing it" is what the drug culture is all about. The drug fiend says, "I sure like those hallucinations of walking on water and thinking I am flying. I'll just take a short cut and rip the veil or insulator between my dream state and this reality. I am going to get high right now."

"Wow!"

What happens if we crack an insulator on a high power transmission line, or we tear the insulation between the opposite electrical poles on our electric-lamp cord? Sparks fly, and the cord burns itself out. Most of us have heard the sayings, "That person fried himself! He had one hit too many! She is burned out!"

They have ripped their veils, so they are seeing bunny rabbits driving cars. We can view this as someone who is uninvited or unprepared trying to sneak in the back door of the wedding feast. Toss them out, and let them fall to the ground until they are straight enough to enter the front door naturally.

Don't fret over this situation. The prodigal child will return home — although it may take a few lifetimes.

Once we know there are other levels of consciousness, we try to find a natural way of maintaining the level we desire without slipping back. We don't want to let two things that are stretched apart with a rubber band just fly back together. Therefore, we don't want to recklessly lacerate our veils, either. We want to atone the opposites back together, slowly.

The dance of the seven veils is a better way to go about removing the camouflage between us and our Creator. We remove the veils layer by layer as we reduce the intensity of our separation. This allows our bodies and consciousness time to adjust to each new vibration of enlightenment as our higher chakras open.

We will not experience the changes in a few moments, as one does on drugs, nor even in a few months, when we remove the veil naturally. But we can look back at ourselves in six months or a year and discern the changes.

What is most rewarding is that all these changes are permanent — as long as we continue moving in a unifying direction. Higher and higher our consciousness spirals as we attune ourselves with the harmony of the universe and the astronomical events that are unfolding.

Now that we have contemplated the philosophical meaning of the Platonic year and understand our position in it, we are going to explore ways to keep the physical temples of our souls in good health through the turning of the ages.

10

Food for Thought

This could be a hard chapter for a lot of us to stomach, but I am going to include it for those of us who are tired of the health conditions on the planet at this time. What follows is my conception of the relationship between foods, health, and the increasing light occurring on the planet at this juncture in the Platonic year. I don't know if this is absolute truth; nevertheless, I have found that it is a good working model for me at this stage of my evolution.

No one can follow precisely in another person's footsteps, although we can learn from one another by observation and communication. Each of us has to follow his or her own path and destiny, yet all paths ultimately lead to the same place. Paths that travel with the astronomical cycles flow much easier than the byways and unreasonable side routes.

Let us describe our existence in the terminology of very general particle physics. We have learned to think of our solar system as composed of particles at a very high vibration. We slow the oscillation of the particles and combine them, as in an erector set, to make our solar system.

The first two elements are *hydrogen* (atomic number 1) and *helium* (atomic number 2). Our sun is primarily made up of these two elements, and it is producing vast amounts of energy in the form of heat and light.

As we slow the particles down, we get *nitrogen* (atomic number 7) and *oxygen* (atomic number 8) in the chemical element table. The air we breathe is chiefly composed of these two elements, and it is very close to the elements of our solar sun in the chemistry chart.

If we combine two hydrogen atoms with one oxygen atom, we create water in our imaginary erector set. The Earth's surface is composed of nearly 75 percent water. In comparison, our bodies are made up of nearly 85 percent water. For the purposes of this life, think of your body as a glass of water from this point onward.

Right in the same area of the element chart is *carbon* (atomic number 6). Plants, being organic as we are, contain carbon as an essential ingredient. Plants turn carbon dioxide into oxygen, and we animals change oxygen into carbon dioxide. Let us explore deeper into the plant family to see how eating the different parts of a plant affect us.

Pretend for a moment that we are walking through a jungle and come upon a fruit-bearing plant. The plant says to us, "Would you please give me a hand by eating some of my fruit and depositing the seeds into the ground? If you grant me this favor, we will produce hundreds more of this fruit for another time you wander by." In effect, the carbon plant asks us to help it. This is a very high and symbiotic relationship.

Let us consider why eating the fruit which the plant produces might be better than eating the plant itself. Some scientists use Kirlian photography to take pictures of plant auras. They have observed that when a person comes into the presence of plants and starts to abuse one plant, the auras of the other plants in the area go into shock. When we love our plants and talk to them, their auras radiate.

Eating the fruit that the plant bears, rather than the plant itself, causes the cells of our bodies to oscillate at a higher vibration. In other words, the energy field that encompasses the living plants we consume creates a template or sets the rate of vibration for the sub-cellular structures of our bodies.

Most traditional or shamanistic belief systems that are designed to reach the higher spiritual levels include fasting on raw fruits and vegetables as an essential practice. Fasting means "getting high" naturally. If we have been fasting on just fruit for a fair amount of time, we may find ourselves dancing around the planet on our toes. So we also eat the roots of the plants, containing starches, to help keep us well grounded.

When we want to eat elements composed of particles at a slower vibration than plants, we can eat another species within our own animal kingdom. If we have been staying attuned to the progressive universities and medical reports, we know that bad cholesterol comes from eating anything with a face or anything that runs from us when we attempt to slaughter it. In today's world, eating fruits and vegetables is becoming the best way to maintain our bodies in excellent condition.

We can also choose to consume some of the heavier elements in our chemistry chart. Ingesting these elements, including aluminum (atomic number 13), chlorine (atomic number 17), and arsenic (atomic number 33), will help plot us in the ground well below the roots of the plants we could be eating.

Remember, none of this has anything to do with good or bad. We are just further down the chemistry element chart. Creation is an amusement, and we can only act within the limits of our erector set.

We are noticing that many of the synthetic or

artificial medications that we are now using have "exposure to sun" alerts on their labels. The natural herbs that doctors have been using for years are not sun reactive, so they don't need these warnings.

When we party too much and throw a lot of junk into our bodies, most of us hide from the sun for the next few days. When we are sick, we shroud ourselves from the sun's energy by pulling down the window shades in our bedroom. On the other hand, if we have been eating only high-vibration foods for a few months, we may find ourselves playing in nature so that we can soak in more solar energy.

Observing when we want to play in the sunlight and when we want to hide from it is important to us at this time in the Platonic year, because the ozone holes are opening and our bodies are being exposed to more light. The word "purity" is involved. When we adulterate the elements, they don't work well in our bodies. The highest rates of skin cancer occur in those countries that are technologically advanced in terms of synthetic foods and medications.

Many scientists are beginning to think that the ozone may be opening up as part of a natural cycle that we don't fully understand. Some of them think that our industrial pollution is not actually the principle agent of this change — it's just hanging around the ozone holes speeding up a natural process.

Many mythologies tell us that the light gets brighter and deserts turn green at this time in the Platonic year. If this prediction turns out to be the truth, then it doesn't matter if the ozone holes are opening naturally or not. We still have to handle more sun.

Each of us has to decide if we want to live shrouded in caves. Or do we want to move up to a higher-vibration food source and spend our lives dancing in the sun?

The medical journals say that cultures that use virgin olive oil experience fewer heart attacks. Virgin olive oil is cold pressed from olives. All we are doing is squeezing the juice out of the olives and using it in our foods.

"Better than Nature's"

We create problems when we change the chemical structure of oil to make it remain more stable so that we can cook at a higher temperature. In that case, we add an extra hydrogen atom to the chemical structure of the oil and, thus, change its natural purity. These kinds of oils are called hydrogenated, or partially hydrogenated, oils.

Purchase any cold or expeller-pressed oil to create a salad. Wash the salad dishes with cold water. The natural oil will just about wash off the dishes without soap. A few hours later, we will notice oil coming out of our pores.

Now try using a partially hydrogenated oil for a salad dressing, and experience washing the dishes in cold water. You'll need to use dish soap and hot water to get the oil off those dishes. A few years later, we have to call "Roto-Rooter" to clean the sink drain.

When we lie out in the sun, we might need to use sun-tanning oil, because a lot of that hydrogenated oil is lining our blood vessels instead of coming out of our pores. Twenty years later we may have to go to the hospital for a roto-rooter job in our bodies.

There is very little difference between our kitchen-sink drains and our glass-of-water bodies. If a food substance we eat isn't washing down the drain effort-lessly, most likely it isn't readily cleansing out of our bodies, either. We may be wearing it to the doctor's office in years to come.

Now, more and more companies are using 100 percent pure-expeller pressing in producing their oils. This means they are mechanically extracting the oils from the raw materials using low heat, and they are not using any unnatural chemical solvents in extracting and refining their oils.

The cognizant salad dressing and potato chip producers are using only cold pressed or expeller-pressed oils in their foods, and they label their products accordingly. Some margarine companies are scrambling to create a non-hydrogenated product; many restaurants are already offering you olive oil as a healthy replacement for margarine or dairy spreads on your bread.

Ultimately, the power for change is in our hands. If we consumers refuse to purchase something, it will no longer be produced.

I am going to share with you how I envision the stages humanity will ascend over many ages as we pass through the Garden of Eden and beyond. The first step we ascertain is that pork and beef are not good for us.

Twenty years ago we thought those far-out vegetarians were crazy, but now we see this knowledge coming up the bell curve as our doctors are finding out that vegetarians who eat pure natural foods are healthier. Deciding to go with the obvious, we give up pork and beef.

As time goes by, we notice that a few of our health-conscious friends are giving up fish and chicken, so we follow along, learning to reduce our intake of these items, when someone comes along and says, "You have been really doing well, but it amazes me that you are still using dairy products. Haven't you noticed that humans are the only animals going from their mother's breast to the cow's tits? All other animals stop suckling dairy products naturally, unless we provide it for them."

"Feel Like Suckling Today?"

A very popular question is, "Where do we obtain our protein if we are not using meat or dairy?" The answer is that we acquire protein from the same plants the vegetarian animals with healthy bones derive it from. We cannot have a protein-deficient diet eating fruits, nuts, and vegetables.

In fact, some doctors believe that the *excess* of protein may be responsible for a lot of our health woes. The universities are beginning to notice that the more protein and dairy one consumes, the higher the levels of osteoporosis. People who eat the most meat and dairy seem to have the worst bones.

For more information concerning the relationship between diets that are based on animal products and maintaining good health, read the book or view the video *Diet for a New America* by John Robbins of the Baskin & Robbins ice cream family.

We have to constantly examine our assumptions. Remember the "four basic food groups" charts that were used for years to teach us proper nutrition in schools? Check out the fine print. You'll discover that many of these subtle advertisements were put out by the meat and dairy industry. Generously enough, they recommended that *half* of our daily food intake be made up of their products.

In 1993, the United States Department of Agriculture replaced the outdated four basic food groups with the new "food guide pyramid," that has wheat, grains, fruits, vegetables, and nuts as the preferred nutritional food sources.

Have you noticed all those big salad bars and vegetarian items that have appeared in the restaurants over the last twenty years? It wouldn't surprise me if one of the major pizza chains catches up with the natural food industry by introducing a soy cheese pizza soon. Most natural food restaurants and stores offer a large variety of soy milk, soy cheeses, and ice-cream substitutes already.

We are beginning to notice that the natural food consumers who haven't ingested any animal products for a long time are starting to look younger. Desiring to be healthier and wanting that face-lift bonus, we aspire to cut out all dairy. We are now "vegans," who don't use any animal products.

Many years or lifetimes pass before someone says, "You have been a good vegan, but why are you eating the roots of the plant? You could be so much lighter if you took the next step and eliminated the roots from your diet." After pondering this for some time, we slowly give up the tubers, giving our bodies plenty of time to adapt to the higher-vibration foods.

Inevitably, some advanced being happens by and asks, "Why is a person like yourself, who is ingesting only the higher foods in the chemistry table of elements, still eating the plant whose aura cringes every time you choose the plant over the fruit it bears? Why aren't you ascending to the original concept of the garden by becoming a fruitarian, who eats just seed-bearing fruits?"

We think, "Why not! I've been reading the Old Testament in my Bible, and it says within the first few pages that we should be fruitarians."

(The appropriate passage is found in Genesis 1:29-31: *God also said; "See, I give you every seed-bearing plant all over the earth and every tree that has seed-bearing fruit on it to be your food; and to all the animals of the land, all the birds of the air, and all the living creatures that crawl on the ground, I give all the green plants for food." And so it happened. God looked at everything he had made, and he found it very good. Evening came, and the morning followed the Sixth Day.*)

We were to be guardians of the animals — not slit their throats and partake in blood rituals. At the end of the Sixth Age, we are verifying that the saying "an eye for an eye" is true. What we are doing to the animals at the slaughterhouse is coming back to haunt us as mastectomies, strokes, heart by-passes, and the many types of cancers we are seeing in our surgery rooms.

"An Eye for an Eye"

Our doctors are beginning to advise us that they are observing a low incidence of heart attacks and cancers in people who are on a natural vegetarian diet. Nevertheless, many of us disregard science, the Bible, and the animals' cries for help; we become addicted to prescription drugs rather then clean up our food intake.

Any time we start putting foods of a higher vibration or purity into our bodies, we can expect a "healing crisis." How many of your friends have said, "I don't understand why I am sick. For the last year or so I have been consuming healthier foods than I've eaten in my entire life"?

A healing crisis could manifest in many ways, including skin eruptions, sore throats, or flu-like symptoms. Some of us stop the natural healing crisis with synthetic medications. After the period it takes our body to recover from the shock of these artificial substances and the residues left by them, we might experience another healing crisis. Some of us repeat the same mistake over and over.

Find yourself a holistic physician who asks you, "What are you doing with your whole life?" We tell him that we have been eating better foods as fast as we can.

The holistic doctor says, "Hold on now! Don't pour a fire hydrant into your glass-of-water body. Do you want to harm yourself detoxifying all at once? It took generations to get this way. Take it easy!"

So we still take medications and have surgery when necessary. We just make more preventive choices. We monitor what we are putting into our glass-of-water bodies, and we learn to differentiate between when we are sick and when we are experiencing an expected healing crisis.

Choose your doctors well, just as you would select a "get well" card. Remember, we begin to look like our mentors if we do everything they do.

Eons have now passed, and we are fruitarians. We have observed and fully comprehend that the Sun God *Ra* and *Raw* Foods are intrinsically interrelated. We are in the garden, and we think no one is ever going to bother us about foods again.

One day, on our way to the beach to bathe *raw* in God's solar energy, we notice a person carrying a sign that reads, "Become a juicearian!" Why are you eating the bag or pulp the juice comes in?

What the heck! Being addicted to getting high and being healthy, we realize that we can get much higher by drinking juice than eating the whole fruit, so we become juicearians.

After a few lifetimes on juice, we meet some far-out person who asks, "Why are you drinking juice? Just drink pure water. The more pure water we put in our bodies, the cleaner and higher we become."

We have been waterarians for many incarnations when some young Einstein asks, "Why are you drinking water? It is such a heavy compound. Water is composed of two hydrogen atoms combined with one atom of oxygen. Why don't you separate those elements and move up the chemistry chart to become breatharians?"

As you might have guessed by now, some stargazing individual comes by a few ages later and asks, "Why are you partaking in oxygen? We can do much better than the rhythm of breathing air. Who needs that cycle? We should be absorbing the light directly from the source. We should all be lightarians."

Guess What! Some alien comes by and says, "Haven't you noticed there are millions of other galaxies in outer space with all their trips? You will also need to give them up one at a time."

Eternity is a long time. The joke of foods is that *you can never get it right!* Once we make one step, there is always another one ahead or behind that one. When we venture out too far ahead of the masses, we are considered to be really crazy, and if we are too far behind them, we are first-class laggards.

Everything is perfect in the universe. We know where we started and where we are going. The fall and the return to the garden are only segments within this Platonic year, or within even greater cycles beyond it. Just go with the flow and maintain an even balance.

I personally made an agreement with my inmost self, the self that causes my sores to heal, controls my organs, and gives me life. I resolved to give it the best foods, water, and air I can procure, and then let it tend to its vocation.

I also made a covenant with the animals not to support the cruelty used in unnecessary medical research, nor to purchase foods or products made from them. Sure I slip! But when I do, I just pick myself up and try again, as it is ultimately all a fun house joke. If we didn't care about our health and the well-being of this planet, we wouldn't be reading this book.

Read *Survival Into the 21st Century* by Viktoras Kulvinskas if you want to know how to look younger, become healthier, understand foods, and get high naturally. It is an exciting and fun book on healing yourself and the planet.

Now that we are beginning to understand the return to the garden which is taking place at the end of the Sixth Age, we are going to cover some odds and ends in the next chapter that will help ease our transition into the coming age.

11

Binding Information

This chapter is going to be a mixed bag of tricks. In other words, anything may pop up that could be a connection to bind or synthesize the information we have pondered already.

Let us start by pretending that our physical bodies are automobiles, vehicles, or vessels. Most of us wouldn't treat our cars the way we treat our bodies — not unless we purchased the car just to run it in the destruction derby next Saturday.

If you enter your car in the destruction derby, what difference does it make if the car comes out of the race a total wreck? The car was acquired for that purpose. We don't expect you to run around asking everyone to repair your car because it is all banged up. No! That would be absurd.

In the same way, you can take your human body and run it through the mill of Earth. Nobody cares!

It is only a vehicle or vessel. Just don't plead and cry, "Fix me!" We take responsibility for our choices.

It is not the world's responsibility to repair any car, or the body, that we deliberately choose to wreck at the destruction derby.

Health care is a joke. Why are we paying for expensive medical treatment for the person who is still being suicidal in the care of his own body? What we really need is more preventive instruction and less synthetic healing.

If we have an old car and we do not know how to drive or maintain it correctly, we can damage the body, brakes, engine, or transmission. Suppose we purchase a new automobile to replace the burned-out vehicle — what makes us think we will perform any healthier with a new one? We would end up destroying the new one, same as the old, because we don't know how to maintain the one we are presently using.

Our source of life is eternal, and we are only where we are. Therefore, it is never too late to change our ways. It doesn't matter how many bodies we go through because ultimately, everything returns to its origin.

I have decided that I don't want to be birthed from a new mummy (Egyptian mummy coffer) right now. I have just earned my freedom from the limitations of childhood, and I have chosen to learn, restore, and play in this body for a while.

Should we decide to restore our old car — our body — we would start by putting good food and oil in it. We would get rid of the fat in our body tissues so the blood can reach the cells and rebuild or replace them. We would cease the abuse of processed sugar and salt that debilitates even the best vehicles.

"To Restore or Not to Restore?"

We might end up with a restored classic automobile, or at least with the knowledge and discipline to maintain our next one. Almost everyone loves a restored classic vehicle, but it is also a great feeling to incarnate in a new one.

If we have a nice sports car, we naturally want to take it out on the roads and see what it will do. We carefully test its limits without damaging or rolling it. We don't leave it parked in the garage, looking all pretty, forever. Take it to the limits! Drive it! Enjoy it! That is what our bodies are for.

Just don't forget: we are responsible for what we do to them.

Now that we have reviewed the mechanical aspects of our physical bodies, let us reflect on some of the philosophical aspects of our being. We will commence with a brief look at some of the more established beliefs.

Some of the Eastern religions believe that God plays all roles. They believe that every person we meet is the Godhead wearing a different mask saying, "Do you want to play with Me?"

In fact, the word *person-ality* is derived from the Italian word *persona*, which refers to the mask worn by the actor to project his voice in a drama.

Jesus said in Matthew 26:40: "*I assure you, as often as you did it for one of my least brothers, you did it for me.*" Does this mean that God is behind every personality or mask? This sounds a lot like the Eastern belief related in a different form or myth.

One way to look at the play of life is to imagine yourself in a fun house with God wearing all the masks. Each disguise asks, "Do you want to play with Me?" The more we play with one persona, the more we look like it. A person only looks greedy until he is no longer miserly.

Once we have had enough, we pick up the pieces of our lives and climb back on the straight and narrow path. Then God just pops out again with a new mask, and most of us are mesmerized into another trip. Behind every mask is God, or our higher self, trying to entrap or captivate us in the universal play.

Should a person ask us to do something that we are not interested in, all we have to say is "No thank you." Just do it with love, because the next being we meet is the same God in another masquerade asking, "Do you want to go to the Synagogue with me?"

Once we finish with a trip, God, who is also our higher self, doesn't try to catch us with that disguise anymore. God puts on another mask, and another, *ad infinitum*, until we wake up and walk out of the fun house.

Let us look at another tale. We are walking on a street, and we see a drunk lying in the gutter. We can go up to God wearing the mask of a drunkard and say, "God! Let me show You how to live."

We could spend the rest of our lives picking alcoholics out of the gutters, or we could walk on by, because the drunk has not asked us for anything. The next being we meet eye to eye will be the same God wearing a different mask, asking if we want to play.

It is very different when the drunk says to us, "I want to talk to you." God wants to talk to us. We have a real problem because God wants to play with us. We reply, "What do you want from me?" The drunk replies, "I want some money to buy some alch... alch... alch... some food! Yes! I need some money to purchase something to eat and *drink*. Ha! Ha!"

We can give the drunk the money, and every time we come down the street the drunkard may think, "Here comes that sucker." Eventually we are taking a different street to avoid giving away our last dollar.

It may be that the drunk really needs money for food. I try to make my decision how to handle this encounter with God personified based on my gut feelings at that moment. We are only playing with our higher selves, and we could make a decision based on emotions that would stifle that person by forestalling her karma.

In other words, we might prevent that person from learning what it feels like to hit rock bottom by continually providing everything she needs to survive.

We could also say to the drunk, "Look at that restaurant across the street. The windows are filthy and the driveway is full of trash. Have you tried going over to the kitchen door and asking if you can clean up the driveway or wash the windows for a sandwich?"

The drunk might pull out a meager roll of money and say, "I do all right here, and I'm free to boot! How much do you make at your witless, enslaving job?" On the other hand, after she thinks about what we said to her, it is also possible that she may get up and walk across the street.

Two weeks later, we might walk by the restaurant and notice that the parking area and windows are clean. Six months later, we notice that the old lush is the dishwasher. A year later, we observe that the drunk is no longer a drunkard. She is bussing tables. Three years later, she is the head waitress, and ten years later, that's her Rolls Royce in front of the restaurant she purchased last year. On top of all of this, we saved a dollar to boot!

Is it that bad to say no? Of course not! "Spare the rod and spoil the child" might be a true statement. We just have to do what we would want done to ourselves in a fair and humane manner. We play with God and solve the riddle of that moment with love.

At this time in the Platonic year, God might be saying, "I am wearing ten masks that represent all the people on Earth. I think I am going to drop a few of my disguises that will not work with the coming of the light or the increasing radiance from the ozone holes. I am going to hang four of these masks up on the wall."

We respond, "No God! I love all your disguises, and I want to save every last one of them."

Allah reassures us, "It is OK. I am just dropping a few of my masks that do not befit the intensity of light that is encompassing the planet during this epoch."

We have to be careful that we don't try to force someone to live the way we think is correct — as long as he or she is not hurting anyone else. Sure it would be nice to have everyone eating natural vegetarian foods and striving to stay healthy, but all we can do is attempt to educate — not force.

You know what I am saying. You can lead a horse to water, but you can't force it to drink. I can't even do all the things that I feel would keep me healthy, so I try not to be to hard on myself, either.

At this era in the Platonic year, God is starting to hang up a few disguises to focus more intensely in fewer masks. I don't even know at what point my guise might not be needed either, and that is all right with me. I am surrendering to the "will" or "universal flow" as much as I am able.

The fun house ride is not over, and I am not going to pretend that I know, at this point, what peek-a-boos are in store for me. I just want to stay attuned and feel love. The function of pain is to nudge us into conforming with the rhythm of the cosmos.

When we have had enough pain in this body, or in a reincarnation of this one, we will transit with the cadence of the creation and its astronomical cycles. In the meantime, I am attempting to frolic through the obviously bizarre manifestations of violent weather and crime taking place on the Earth at this juncture of ages.

Imagine a burglar caught in the act by someone shining a flashlight. The intruder usually goes berserk. Notice the dementia on the planet with the slight increase of light we are now experiencing. Do not resist what is taking place on the planet Earth at this time in the Platonic year. Let the light do its work. It is only Ra dropping a few masks.

We move up the hill if the water is rising in our area. Likewise, we change our own body's vibration if we want to handle the intensifying light. The new pulsation levels anything that is not attuned to it, just as a singer's high-pitched note shatters a glass.

Some of my fundamentalist Christian friends assure me that Jesus's light is much brighter than the sun. I can agree with that statement as a parable. I just reply, "Yes, His radiance is much brighter than the Earth's measly old sun, but if we can't handle this sun and we are looking for anything brighter, we are going to get fried."

The sun will tan us and make us healthy or it will tan our asses, as fathers do occasionally. We have to proceed from where we are. A good place to begin is with this little old sun. Moving back into the garden and setting the animals on this planet free is also another way to start our adjustment to the increasing light in this particular body.

We are beginning to notice an increasing rate of animal extinction taking place on Earth at this juncture in the Platonic year. I hope that the increasing light will be enough to take out the mosquitoes, fire ants, and other masks of God that make any return to the garden unpleasant, but fossils that we have found from previous Platonic years indicate that they will most likely survive.

Remember Genesis 1:30: *"For all the animals of the land, all the birds of the air, and all the living creatures that crawl on the ground, I give all the Green Plants for food."* I wish they would stick to eating plants instead of us.

How would I know what's going on? I am no further along than anyone else. I am right here on Earth. I am making revel of it, because the play of life is unfolding just as it is written in all the mythologies. Why should we be so mystified by the grotesque events that are taking place on the planet?

The Bible and the sacred writings or scriptures of many people in the world say it all gets *hide*ous at this time in the great year. If that's the case, then why are we pleading for duped people to send or give more money to stop the *mazzaroth*? Are we trying to prove the Sacred Books wrong?

"We Need to Raise More Money"

Are we not tired of building mansions? Give to the poor, help your neighbor, and do unto others and the animals as you would have done unto yourselves, without being foolish.

If Revelations says this is the way it happens, why not revel, celebrate, and enjoy life with the produce from the garden, as everything is perfect in the universe? Only a person who is deep in the Piscean maze could still believe that one hand of God wins over the other hand of the same God.

As we enter the Aquarian age, many of us are realizing how ridiculous, yet stimulating, this belief was. Yet, even more amusing is the realization that it is *necessary* to believe that one fish wins over the other fish just to play.

The Piscean outlook caused us to fret and worry, because the more we tried to make good win over evil, the more evil we had to contend with. At this time in the Platonic year, a rejuvenating consciousness is springing up within and around us that is replacing the antiquated ideas of the previous ages.

Remember the fall of the beast! The Fall or Autumn is going into the beast or lion at this time, and Spring, or new beginnings, is dawning into man. Just keep attuning slowly.

Let us look at the creation of the universe as related in the following allegory. The Oneness constructs a very large roller coaster. God gets on the roller coaster and comes down the first large dip. Ra's stomach is in its throat. Allah forgets it built the roller coaster or cosmos, because universal consciousness can only focus on surviving the rush of the first plunge.

As the roller coaster ride continues, the dips begin to unify as they become smaller. Adoan'i is yelling! "What a creation this roller coaster is! Scared the heck out of Me! I love it!" The Oneness purchases another ticket.

The foregoing allegory sounds like Buddha's famous saying, "Desire is the Creator."

At this time in the Platonic year, Mother Nature awakens and starts to balance, raze, or level everything discordant with the coming of the new Aeon. She is saying to us, "Come out of the fun house! Get off that roller coaster! Come out of the carnival! Enough of this bazaar! It is time to start heading h*ome*."

"What do you Desire?"

We are pleading like little kids. "Please Mom! One more ride on the roller coaster! Please! Can we dawdle just a few more hours at the carnival?"

Mother Nature is saying, "Father is coming! Can't you see the light increasing? Ra is coming! Do you want to get your behinds tanned, or are we going to initiate heading home? The workmen want to dismantle this carnival so the grass and plants in the field can start growing again. The weight of this Piscean Circus is killing them."

To attempt to buck the flow of nature at this time is only to increase the amount of disease and pain we are experiencing.

Let us commence the closure of this chapter with a few bits of related information.

We will start with the letter "G", a primeval symbol which represents the spiraling Milky Way Galaxy, or the root of sacredness for many civilizations around the world.

In the Mayan culture, the symbol "G" represents the beginning. It is the essence, core, or seed from which all life springs. The "G" represents the spin of our Milky Way Galaxy. The "G" is one of the oldest symbols we know of, and is found on a majority of the Mayan ruins.

The Mayan word *ge* means zero, aura, essence, egg, or the Milky Way. We find many of their words in the languages of Europe and Asia.

Read *Secrets of Mayan Science / Religion* by Hunbatz Men for more information on this subject.

The letter "J" was introduced much later in history. It was originally identical with the Roman "I" until the seventeenth century when it was made a consonant and separate letter of our alphabet. We still say ge-sus or Jesus. Ge-sus is the Milky Way galaxy including our solar Sun.

Who created it? You pick the word or sound for the whole that suits your mythology.

We also discern that the words "whole" and "hole" are intrinsically tied together in form and space — like the *whole* material universe with its black *holes*.

Even the word *religion* is derived from the Latin expression *religare*, meaning to reunite. The whole idea of religion is reuniting, rather than keeping the Whole, the Oneness, or God separated indefinitely in duality. It may be time for those of us who are teaching the concept of heaven opposing hell to begin the process of unifying the Whole or God by perceiving and revealing the truth.

"Let Me See"

Even though my veil is thinning, I don't stand a chance at this period in the Platonic year to figure it all out. It is a mystery to me. I only travel through life looking for pieces of the puzzle. I am sharing with you how I have the pieces placed at this time. They could all be wrong. I keep adapting according to what is revealed to me in truth.

Realizing that visible bodies are only symbols of invisible forces, I view my body as my spirit at a lower vibration, and it reflects everything I am. The belief that material and spirit are separate is a holdover from the Piscean Age.

Water is ice at a lower vibration, and it is steam at a high vibration. Even though we change the vibration, it is still what it is. It has only changed form.

At one time in the Platonic year there was only one page in the Bible. As history progressed, a few more chapters were added. After Jesus resurrected, there were more chapters added. What makes us think what we are doing today isn't the next chapter in the eternal play of Ah?

Speaking of next chapters, there are some ancient-mythological creatures waiting to share with us a timely symbol that is very revealing. Therefore, when you feel ready, let us move on.

12

Removing the Shroud

Well, my friends and co-conspirators in life, it is time to pull this book together. Let us start by looking at the dot — a minute point, speck, or round mark. The dot is the symbol for the origin of the material plane, and it also represents the material creation pulled back into its source. The dot is characterized by the number zero.

●

Dot

Next we have the expansion of the dot into the perfect circle. We now have the form of the circle and the space within it giving us a symbolic representation of matter and space. All structure comes forth and evolves into the circle that has no beginning or end.

Perfect Circle

The perfect circle depicts the "whole of creation," or the hole left by the emergence of form from it. Its mystery is unity, and its number is nine.

When we take two dots and connect them, we get a line that represents the balance of the two opposites or the oneness of duality. The line signifies union that is on the path towards unity. Its number is two, because it takes two points or opposing poles to make a number one or line.

Line

For example, we can only look into one set of eyes at a time, and when we go eye to eye with another being for any length of time, many magical things happen. We start to sense union on a visual plane.

If we place three points an equal distance apart and connect them with three lines, we construct an equilateral triangle, or a plane that has no depth. The triangle is the symbolic representation of the mystic Trinity. It is the two opposites in union with themselves and with the Creator in its own creation.

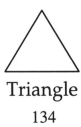

Triangle

The triangle is free from suffering because the creation has not yet descended into the depth of the material plane.

When we place four dots an equal distance apart from each other, we can connect them as a square that represents a solid foundation, or we can construct them into a tetrahedron that is a solid bounded by four plane triangular faces. Four gives us the ability to experience dimensions with depth. Once we expand into depth, we can start to experience pain and suffering.

Square and Tetrahedron

When we center the dot, or point, within the circle, we produce one of the universal symbols for our sun. It also represents our sun as the dot, with the Zodiac and its twelve constellations depicted by the circle.

Symbol for the Sun

Let us remove the first layer of the shrouded riddle by placing the square representing the four primary forces or pillars of the heavens in the circle depicting the Zodiac. When we connect the four corners or dots of the square, we produce a cross in a circle, or square.

Each of the four elements, consisting of earth, fire, air, and water, are represented by the constellations that the four ends of the cross point to, and they are in perfect balance with one another.

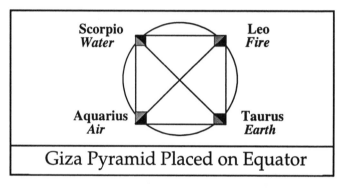

Giza Pyramid Placed on Equator

For the purpose of discussion, let us view the above diagram as the Great Pyramid of Giza expanded to the size of half the Earth, and we are looking down on it. The circle portrays the Equator, and the four corner sockets of the Pyramid are overhanging it.

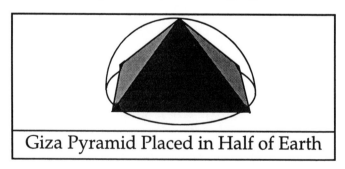

Giza Pyramid Placed in Half of Earth

The fundamental unit of measurement which the builders of the Great Pyramid used in its construction was the pyramid inch. It is equal to 1.001 of our inches. The diagonals of the base of the Giza Pyramid measure approximately 12,913 pyramid inches each. Many scholars believe this figure represents half of the 25,800 years in the precession of the equinoxes or Platonic year.

We have examined the square in the Zodiac in Chapter Seven of this book, so let us focus our attention on three dots placed in the configuration of an equilateral or mystical triangle. Place that triangle in the Zodiac.

Assign one of the dots of the triangle to represent the Spring Equinox, and position it in the Age of Pisces. This is the constellation the sun has been traversing for the last 2,000 years.

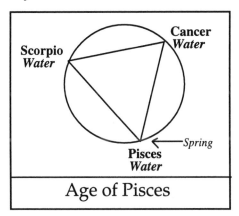

We will find one of the two remaining points in Cancer, that represents the vermin or scarab carrying the sun through the night.

The last point of the triangle is in Scorpio, whose poisonous sting causes death, or the release of the soul to soar like an eagle. All three of these constellations are symbolized by the element of *water*.

If I were to summarize the Age of Pisces relative to the Biblical stories, I would say that the Sun was traveling in the waters of the lower world. This is represented by the Fisherman who died on the cross. We have been traveling in darkness waiting for the return of the Sun or enlightenment so that mankind can soar once again into the heavenly air with wings like an eagle.

If we place the triangle at our current juncture in the Platonic year, the point representing the Vernal Equinox is dawning into the Age of Aquarius.

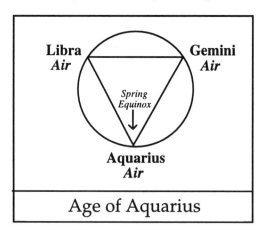

As we can plainly see, one of the two remaining points of the triangle is in Gemini, that represents Adam and Eve, balance, or union of the two.

The last point is in the constellation of Libra that depicts a woman holding a set of scales from her hand. Libra, like Gemini, also signifies balance of the opposites or justice. Notice that all three points of our triangle are now in the constellations representing the element of *air*.

If I had to summarize the dawning into the Age of Aquarius, I would say that mankind starts to comprehend the oneness of all life and that the opposite polarities go together. Hence, we began the process of unifying our beings.

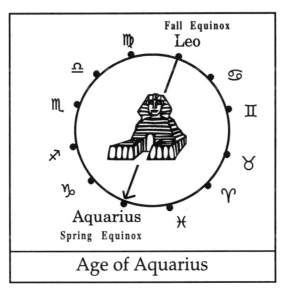

Age of Aquarius

Now that we have looked at the square made of four dots and the triangle created with three dots, let us move our attention to the two dots that construct a number one when they are connected by a line.

Place the line in the Zodiac so that it connects the points representing our present Vernal and Autumnal Equinoxes. The line will connect the Spring Equinox going into Aquarius the Man with the Fall Equinox going into Leo the Lion. These are the same two points that the Giza Sphinx, with the head of a man and body of a lion, binds together. This also symbolizes Leo the Lion heralding the awakening and coming into being of mankind. (See diagram on page 139.)

Let us turn the line back into the constellations that the equinoxes are departing at this juncture in the Platonic year. We now have the Spring point of the line located in Pisces the Fish and the Fall point in Virgo the Virgin. Replace the male Sphinx with the *Ancient Mermaid*. Place her head in Virgo and her tail in Pisces. The Mermaid now connects the Fisherman of Pisces with his Virgin Mother in the ancient legends.

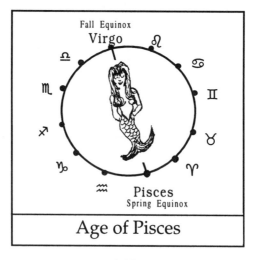

Age of Pisces

The desired son and the virgin are found in many world savior mythologies from Krishna and his Hindu mother Devaki, Horus and his Egyptian mother Isis or Aspolia, Ieza or Christos and his Greek mother Ceres, to Jesus and his Virgin mother Mary, just to mention a few.

As you may recall from Chapter Five, we found the female appearance of the Giza Sphinx in an Egyptian Zodiac binding Virgo and Leo. Let us allow the Mermaid, the male aspect of the Giza Sphinx, and the female guise of that same Sphinx to take their positions in the Zodiac. Now they are in position to bring to life their enshrouded partner by removing the veil between Aquarius and Pisces.

Oh My God! We have *revealed* the most ancient and Sacred Being, whose time has come. His shroud is now scattered throughout the pages of this book, our souls, and the universe. We have the Ancient Merman or the Fisherman who guides us through the Golden Age, or Millennium, that occurs between the sixth and seventh ages.

The Babylonians called the coupled signs of Pisces and Aquarius the Fish-Man. The Chaldeans, who conquered and ruled Babylon, tell us about Oannes, the Merman, who came out of the Red Sea and taught the people along the shore to plant seeds and harvest the fruits. He also instructed them in reading, writing, astronomy, herbs for healing, geometrical principles, governing with laws, and understanding the Sacred Mysteries.

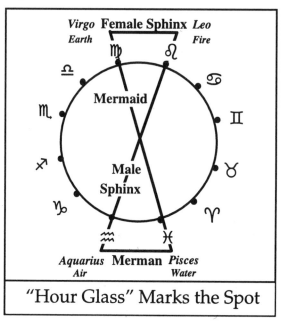

Virgo **Female Sphinx** *Leo*
Earth ♍ ♌ *Fire*
♎
♏ **Mermaid** ♊
♐ **Male Sphinx** ♉
♑ ♈
♒ ♓
Aquarius **Merman** *Pisces*
Air *Water*

"Hour Glass" Marks the Spot

Read *The Secret Teachings of All Ages,* by Manly P. Hall, for much more fascinating information on Oannes and other shamanistic stories from the Mayan culture and the American Indians that tell us of real or mythological men rising from the waters to teach the people the lost knowledge of Atlantis, Lemuria, or Mu. This book also provides information about the Fish-Man teachers in ancient Hinduism, Buddhism, Paganism, and the more recent parables of Christianity and the Islamic Koran.

We now have the Mermaid binding Virgo and Pisces, the male aspect of the Giza Sphinx binding Aquarius and Leo, the female aspect of that same Sphinx binding Virgo and Leo, and the Merman binding Pisces and Aquarius. When all of these ancient beings come together in their proper places in the Zodiac, they construct an *Hour Glass* that marks the rapidly approaching millennium, or Golden Age of this Platonic year.

It would be hard for me to express what vibrations I am sensing at this very moment. My fingers are on the keyboard, and energy is rising up my spine, as this chapter is being written before my very own eyes. I have expressed already that we are creating this book together. I am only an instrument to reaffirm in simple, clear words what a great number of us are already sensing.

It is time for all of humanity to prepare for the New Age by realizing that one mythology is not superior to another. The Lion, whose element is fire, is heralding in the new Aeon by burning up the antiquated interpretations of all our religious beliefs.

We celebrate the *New Year* every January 1 to mark the astronomical event of 365 days. We let go of each year by throwing our old calendars out the windows of high rise buildings around the world. It may be time for the masses to start throwing out their previous age calendars and to commence celebrating the celestial event of the new Aquarian Age and the midway point of this Platonic year.

This is a golden opportunity for our astrologers, astronomers, universities, broadcast media, map-makers, and legislators to unite and reconcile us with the astronomical reality of our times. It is time to put the Piscean belief that one side wins over the other behind us as the unifying force of the Aquarian Age engulfs us.

It is also time to rename the Tropic of Cancer and the Tropic of Capricorn on our maps and globes to the Tropic of Taurus and the Tropic of Scorpio. Even astrology needs to update all of its charts and data to reflect our current position in this great year. This should help us and our descendants move into this new era with a viable perspective. Very few of our religious or sacred symbols will ever make sense until the consciousness of this planet awakens enough to attune our data with reality.

Think of this challenge as a means of making the planet a place we would like to revisit, a place our offspring would find in harmony. We only have a few years left in our individual lives; we could leave a legacy as the generation that synchronized us with the Platonic year for the next 2,000 years. After all, the process of change will go on, whether we unite with Mother Nature in making these necessary alterations or not.

As I stated earlier in this book, Adam and Eve birthed us into the Age of Gemini, Moses kicked us into the Aries Age, Jesus hooked us into the Piscean Age, and we are going to deliver us into the light of the Aquarian Age.

Even though the festivities for observing a new age should be unforgettable, it is almost unimaginable what the celebration for the halfway-turning point of this Platonic year might involve. As we have seen throughout this book, there are countless ancient ruins and legends all over the planet Earth marking this for us.

In the next chapter, we are going to create our own model of Revelations, and we will look at what changes we might expect the Earth to encounter at this time in the Platonic year.

145

Beware

Chapter *13* is Fiction

13

Beyond the Twilight Zone

T hink of the Sun and its twelve constellations, Jacob and his twelve sons, and Jesus and the twelve apostles; the number of main characters adds up to the infamous number *thirteen*. I felt playful enough to follow that archetypal pattern, and to include one chapter laden with visionary prophecy to balance this work.

I found a book that allowed me to harmonize a few discordant revelations from my strong Christian programming with the realities of our present times. I revised and condensed a small part of this 1950 publication called "The Impending Golden Age" by Sanctilean, so that we could create a model of the millennium that may be a *step* closer to actuality than some of the archetypes many of us have been exposed to in this lifetime.

I neither believe nor disbelieve the following information, although I do find it thought-provoking. We can only wait until someone creates a better model or time reveals the truth.

Some of my close friends cautioned me that including this chapter, which is based on an idea that can't be proven by astronomers, could debase the factual information contained in the rest of this book. I believe that you are shrewd enough not to let my experiment in prophecy and the use of a hypothetical model for the orbits of our celestial bodies mislead you down that incongruous path.

We are going to be playing, one step beyond the twilight zone, on a level that doesn't exist in some structures. Enjoy!

The progression of souls on every plane of creation is concordant with the astronomical cycles of our universe. Moons revolve around planets that are orbiting their sun. At the same time, solar systems course about stars of different wavelengths that rotate around other suns that spin around the center of our spiral galaxy.

Sanctilean would say that a Platonic year equals one elliptical orbit of our solar system about a hypothetical central sun henceforth called *Vela*. This theoretical star is not discernible to us, because its radiation lies in wavelengths beyond the perception of our senses.

The orbits of the many solar systems that course our central sun are very elongated. At one point in our sun's orbit we are closer to Vela. This causes our sun to shine with a brilliant blue-white light containing a large amount of ultraviolet radiation. When our solar system is at its farthest point from Vela, our sun's light fades to a dull red color, and it emits less ultraviolet radiation.

A Platonic year begins when our sun, having reached the most remote point in its orbit about the central sun, begins its progression towards it. This would have been around 13,000 years ago when we dawned the Age of Leo.

At the opposite point in this long orbit, close to this theoretical star, prior to receding from it, we are immersed in its golden aura. A Golden Age begins the moment that our solar system enters the central sun's radiation, and it ends when we emerge from it.

Sanctilean estimates that this Golden Age will be approximately 880 years in length, and we will be closest to Vela at the midway point of this age. Therefore, any polarity reversals or major planetary shifts, should they occur as a natural function of this cycle, would be nearly 440 years away, even though rapid changes of the Earth's surface start as we enter this mini age.

The Golden Age occurs between the Piscean and Aquarian ages in the Platonic year. When one counts this age as a solar age, we end up with some people quoting *thirteen* ages in a Platonic year.

According to Sanctilean, errors in translation caused us to apply the word *millennium* to this middle age of a Platonic year. Prophetic authors, accordingly, have supposed that the impending millennium will be one thousand years in length.

Some other inaccuracies being professed by many of our present-day theologians is that millenniums are not recurrent, and that the impending one will mark the end of the human race on Earth, if not the planet itself. Some humans have a tendency to personalize cosmic verities and to project images of violence and disaster into the orderly process of cosmic actuality.

At the conclusion of each solar cycle of progress, because there is a methodical and irrevocable uplifting of the whole solar system during the millennium, everything exists upon a higher level of spiritual excellence. The cosmic principle of progression will not allow any permanent degeneration of the universe or of its inhabitants. Progress may be impeded, but it cannot be reversed by any act of man. The ways of the cosmos are above human meddling.

In Sanctilean's model of the 25,800 year cycle of the Earth, an era of civilization is called an "enascium". The words "enascium" and "nascent" are derived from the obsolete word *enascant* that means *coming into being*. The first solar age of an enascium starts at the end of the millennium or the beginning of the seventh age of a Platonic year. The last of the twelve solar ages that make up an enascium is the sixth solar age of the existing Platonic year. An enascium is "one act" in the human drama of becoming.

A Golden Age is not part of the twelve ages making up an enascium. This mini age is the veil between two of Sanctilean's enasciums. It is similar to a bar between two measures of time in a piece of music. The most recent bar is the veil of antiquity that hangs so darkly between our present enascium and the knowledge from a previous one.

The prehistoric groups who emerged from behind this veil carried over the cultural values distilled from within the violence that gathered around the last days of the preceding enascium. Because we can't penetrate this veil, we entertain many mistaken beliefs with respect to the past and the future of physical and spiritual life.

Occasionally a highly evolved soul incarnates on the physical plane to reaffirm publicly the ancient teachings concerning liberation. Jesus was not a sacrificial lamb who died to atone for man's sins, nor for the transgressions of the world. He embodied in order to demonstrate the way of purity, sobriety, altruism, and non-resistance to evil, even unto death. He showed us by example the path of freedom, and he proclaimed to all the world, "What I do, you shall do also."

The practice of shedding of blood in animal and human sacrifice has led man continuously into war, pestilence, disease, and death throughout the ages. Being humanly created, any prophecy that affirms sacrifice or vengeance is inaccurate. Distortion of authentic prophecy, as revealed in the sacred writings, is the result of human tampering — mistakes by copyists, forgeries, ignorance, or dishonest propaganda for selfish religious, political, or racial purposes.

Our sun's energy is affected by its proximity to our central sun. As we approach Vela, the infrared rays of our sun diminish in intensity, and the ultraviolet rays increase in strength.

The infrared rays are the thermal rays, and as they decrease, sunshine will possess less heat. The Earth will become cooler, though the danger of sunburn will increase due to the intensifying ultraviolet rays. Desert areas will become habitable because of the lower temperatures and increased rainfall.

This almost sounds like our present-day ozone openings.

The density of the electromagnetic force field of any astronomical body is greatest near the surface of the body and least near the periphery of its aura. As our solar system approaches the central sun at this time in the Platonic year, it moves rapidly into the denser portions of Vela's electromagnetic force field.

This change in the density develops ethereal vortices in the Earth's own electromagnetic force field, which become physically manifest as tornadoes of increasing frequency and violence.

The last days of every enascium are accompanied by earthquakes and storms. They are the precursors of the more rapid changes that remodel the surface of the Earth at the beginning of every Golden Age.

"Looks Like Changes to Me"

Immediately following the major renovation of the planet during a millennium, the Earth is renewed and ready for a new act in the human drama of becoming. The finest souls embody on the Earth's surface to commence a new enascium. They come from the highest level of vibration attained in their post-mortem existence upon supra-physical planes. Less mature souls, from successively lower levels of vibration, incarnate from that time forward through the twelve solar ages of the enascium.

Reincarnation is an aspect of the recurrent cycle of lowering and lifting a soul through its gamut of vibrations. The attributes of an individual's personality are a direct reflection, in the physical world, of the deeds of the individual's soul.

During the last days of an enascium, the most lagging souls embody among the many evolving beings on the surface of the Earth. Some of these laggards manifest mental, moral, or spiritual deviations. It is the unethical souls who contribute the most to the social chaos and violence in the closing days of an enascium. They are found in every aspect of life, including the religious, the national, the racial, and the economic.

Even this chaos and violence, however, are a part of the operation of cosmic law with respect to all evolving life. We should not resent or combat the evil of these last days. We should aspire to understand the verities, principles, and laws of cosmic actuality that are in full control of today's events. When we tire of the turmoil in our lives, we will strive daily to attune ourselves to cosmic reality.

It is a known fact that light causes growth in plants, animals, and man. A plant that is shut away from the light will wither and die. The sun's radiation can be invigorating and healthful, or it can burn us. Radiation that is beyond the wavelength of visible light is also active in producing development, but it can increase evil as well as good.

The light flowing from a highly spiritual being will so illuminate the evil in those of low spirituality that they will appear to become even more baneful than before. Often when a compassionate soul attempts to help a vile person, he or she will only increase the discordance in the unfortunate being. This causes sorrow not only for the fallen soul but also for the one who seeks to reclaim him.

Thus, ironically, the first effect of an increased inflow of spiritual light is to augment the evil. This is one of the reasons why Arisen Masters are so hard to find. They avoid close contact with impure humans so that their great radiance shall not injure them. If we want to contact an Arisen Master, we first must purify ourselves physically, emotionally, and mentally.

Today our solar system is moving rapidly into the fringe of Vela's radiation, and this radiation is amplifying the disharmony in the spiritual laggards who are coming into embodiment. The ultra*violet* radiation is causing these laggards to be more *violent* than they would be otherwise.

Nature has brought these souls into an environment of rapidly increasing vibrations, in which their inharmonious desires and criminal tendencies are so enhanced that they are driven to all types of crimes and aberrations.

This is the process of their cleansing, as drastic as it may be. It is the lash of cause and effect, as there is no other remedy for the misdeeds of these baneful humans. The karma of their transgressions cannot be assumed vicariously by another, and the release from censures cannot be purchased by tithes or by clergy absolutions. The saying "God helps those who help themselves" is befitting here.

For many humans, the black and sour fruits of many discordant lives are slowly being consumed in the increasing radiance of the central sun Vela, which burns ever more intensely toward the close of an enascium. Today, the healing light flows most purely into thinly populated and desert areas, while psychic confusion becomes overwhelming in the densely populated areas.

As Vela's aura slowly engulfs our solar system, it burns within and around everything on Earth. Humans will discover themselves immersed in flame-like radiance. If they are attuned with the flow of the astronomical cycles, this fire will not burn their flesh. The consuming of disharmony will be almost indescribably refreshing.

156

For bodies filled with physical, emotional, and mental impurities, the radiation will be painful or fatal during the bathing in the lake of fire. The diseased beings are becoming loudly vocal as they are cleansed by the increasing radiation. Their refusal to flow with the harmony of the universal truths justifies our labeling them as ignorant, since they are ignoring the signs of the times.

As the smoke from the consuming clears, the remaining humans will discover a renewed Earth around them, and the Arisen Masters will no longer be hidden from their sight. Only then, in the silence that follows, will humanity realize the oppression it suffered in that psychic turmoil it formerly endured.

Cleansed of the accumulated psychic emissions of the current enascium, the Earth will enter the Golden Age. The descendants of the survivors will go on to create the next race to emerge from behind the approaching veil in the musical dance of the spiraling cosmos.

As I reflect on civilization's odyssey from the Age of Leo to the end of the Piscean Age, I keep asking myself if the legend of "Jason and the Argonauts" doesn't foreshadow this whole journey.

Jason and his fellow travelers set sail from the constellation of Argo, which is a part of Cancer, to reclaim the golden fleece that had been lost. The main sail of their ship, the Argo, is the constellation of Vela.

Is this story a revelation about setting sail from the start of this Platonic year to reclaim ourselves in the Golden Age? Do we then *desire* to lose ourselves in the play again? Is existence on the material and astral planes just an act in the drama of eternal life?

Jason and the Argonauts Set Sail

My friends, I don't have all the answers. I am only sharing with you how I have placed some pieces of the universal puzzle at this time, using the Zodiac as the border of this great enigma.

As you combine this information with the knowledge you have previously acquired, you become the teachers once again, because you now know what little I know plus all that you know. That makes you smarter than I.

We could go on and on, but this must go to press before some of us make a transition by exiting this stage. Let each of us take a picture of this moment in eternity and print it correctly on our maps, globes, and astrological charts.

Let us also update our interpretation of the myths, legends, and folklore from ancient times to reflect our present understanding of the universe. This should help us and our descendants make more sense out of our religious beliefs, for they are relative to these times.

Remember, even though I may not always show it, I love you in all ways.

Selected Bibliography

Be assured that the *Secrets of the Sphinx* contains a lot of original material that you will not find in any of the following sources, but you will find bits and pieces of information that led me to create this book. The sources that have been important to me at one time or another in my life have an asterisk * preceding them.

* Anonymous, *The Impersonal Life* (De Vorss Co. 1941-1969)
* Anonymous, *The Living Light* (J. F. Rowny Press 1951)
* Baba Ram Dass, *Be Here Now* (Crown Publishing 1971)
  Bok, Bart and Priscilla, *The Milky Way* (Harvard University Press 1981)
  Bulinger,E. W., *The Witness of the Stars* (Kregel Publications 1967)
* Carey, Ken, *Starseed Transmissions* (Harper-San Francisco)
* Capt, Raymond, *The Glory of the Stars* (Artisan Sales 1976)
  Capt, Raymond, *The Great Pyramid Decoded* (Artisan Sales 1991)
* Churchward, Colonel J., *The Lost Continent of Mu* (Ives Washburn 1931)
  Cousto, Hans, *The Cosmic Octave* (Life Rhythm 1987)
  Crowley, Aleister, *The Book of Thoth* (Samuel Weiser 1989)
  Edgar, Morton, *The Great Pyramid - Its Scientific Features* (Glasgow 1924)
  Gurshtein, Alex A., *On the Origin of the Zodiacal Constellation* (Pergamon)
* Hall, Manly P., *Secret Teachings of All Ages* (Philosophical Research 1978)
* Hesse, Hermann, *Siddhartha* (Bantam Press)
  Kippenhahn, Rudolf, *100 Billion Suns* (Basic Books Inc. 1983)
* Kulvinskas, Viktaras, *Survival into the 21st Century* (Omangod Press 1975)
  Lemesurier, Peter, *The Great Pyramid Decoded* (Elements Books 1989)
  Lewis, Richard S, *The Illustrated Encyclopedia of the Universe* (Harmony)
* Long, Max Freedom, *The Secret Science at Work* (De Vorss Co. 1943)
  Men, Hunbatz, *Secrets of Mayan Science/Religion* (Bear & Co. 1990)
  Norelli-Bachelet, Patrizia, *Symbols and the Question of Unity II* (Servire)
* Robbins, John, *Diet for a New America* (Stillpoint Publishing. 1987)
* Sanctilean, *The Impending Golden Age* (J. F. Rowny Press 1950)
  Seiss, Joseph A., *The Gospel in the Stars* (Kregel Publications 1972-1982)
* Spaulding, Barid T., *Life and Teachings of the Masters of the Far East*
    (De Vorss 1924-1964)
  Unger's Bible Dictionary (Moody Press, Chicago)